Best Wishes Pastor Bonnie !

Laurent Muvunyi

VOICE OF CENTRAL AFRICA
DEMOCRATIC REPUBLIC OF CONGO

BY
DEBRA LYNN HEAGY

WITH
LAURENT MUVUNYI

Xulon PRESS

Voice of Central Africa DR Congo
by Debra Lynn Heagy with Laurent Muvunyi

Printed in the United States of America

ISBN 9781619044500

www.xulonpress.com

Table of Contents

Preface

Debra Lynn Heagy

S aturday night in January of 2009, Rex and I met Laurent and John Paul at our evening service at Marshall Road Church of God. We greeted and talked with them as we always do with new people. We started the Saturday evening service in hopes of reaching the community of people who work on Sundays. These two special people really needed our help and guidance.

In 2009, I prayed to the Lord to help me grow spiritually by serving in a ministry. Rex, my husband, lost his dad due to esophageal cancer, and we both needed something positive in our lives. Rex wanted to become a part-time pastor and needed to take steps to solidify that desire. The Saturday night services needed pastors, and it seemed a perfect place for Rex to start.

The following Sunday service I met one of John Paul's family members, Joyeuse, who was starting classes at Fairmont High School. I noticed her right hand and wrist were swollen, and she did not have full range of motion. I asked her what happened to her arm. She told me it was a "gunshot wound" and added, "I was shot in Gamutumba Refugee Camp in Burundi."

Her brief story sparked in me the idea for a book. I have worked on two children's books previously and gone through several writers' workshops in writing stories. In the meantime, this family needed our help as a church to get established in the Kettering area. Laurent's wife, Nicole, was nine months pregnant. The church pulled together needed food and household items, and the young family was so appreciative. Rex and I helped where we could, and I assisted them with their English. The children on John Paul's side of the family needed help with their English and understanding instructions in their homework. My mother also helped out in donating some household items for their apartment.

The answer to prayer was these two young men from Africa and the needs for their families. One night I had a dream of a book with a tree in the bright-orange sky. I thought of a book with a collection of testimonies from the survivors of the Gatumba genocide. But from the dream, the territory had to cover a larger area of Africa, and Central Africa would cover people from Rwanda, Burundi, and the Congo who have experienced genocide at Gatumba or other massacres in this area.

The other request came to me in an audible voice from the Lord that there needed to be at least 100 testimonies to make a difference in the lives of these people. Thus, the title of the book is *Voice of Central Africa*. I shared this dream and book idea with Laurent, and thus the project began. I thought of at least seven questions to ask about their personal lives, Christian lives, and specifically about their own personal experience with genocide/massacre and how it affected their own lives and families. I encouraged them to tell me their stories. I asked Laurent, Nicole, Paul (the one I helped on his homework and English skills), as well as Joyeuse. Then over the weeks and months names and very interesting stories emerged one at a time.

In a testimony by Pastor Adrien Kajabika, he stated he had a dream about this book. It's very moving to me how God joined Pastor Adrien Kajabika and me in our dream for this book at the same time. I thank the Lord for this special request and His faith in me to write this book.

I thank my husband, Rex, and my daughter, Jennifer, for their love and understanding through this whole project. I also thank my mother for her love and encouragement. My mother had fallen in the spring and had other health challenges, but we came through each event with grace. I had a loving family and church family as well as the Banyamulenge people here and in Africa who prayed for my family. I thank Pastor Kevin Hall from our church, who prayed and visited me and Mother at the hospital on several occasions.

I am so thankful to God that he has extended my family to include Laurent, Nicole, and their son, Grant. We welcome them to our family. We are their "American Mom and Dad." I helped in the delivery of their firstborn son on April 21, 2009 at 6:30 p.m. I had the honor of cutting the umbilical cord. He is a very healthy boy who was born in Dayton, Ohio, at Miami Valley Hospital. I thank Laurent and Nicole for their love, understanding, and patience during the long hours of all the testimonies and translation issues we encountered.

I thank the Banyamulenge people for having faith and trust in me and taking the time to share their miracles, joys, fears, and tragedies. This book, in time, will let the world know about all the genocides and massacres these people have experienced and are still experiencing today in Central Africa.

Laurent Muvunyi

My name is Laurent Muvunyi. I was born in a small village called Mukato, Rurambo, in South Kivu province in the DRC, formerly Zaire.

My father, Mashavu B., is a retired pastor from the Assemblies of God Church in the Hauts Plateaux of Uvira. He was ordained a pastor in 1946. His entire career was a firm commitment to serve God.

I had a dream of writing a book in 2002 when I was in business school at Ngozi University in Burundi. I immediately called my friend, Roland Runezerwa, and shared my vision with him. At that time I didn't have all the resources.

In 2003, I the same dream came to me again. In 2004 right after the Gatumba genocide, my heart was pushing me to do something so that the world may know what happened.

In July 2008 when I was sleeping in my bedroom, in my dreams, I saw a man.

He woke me up and asked me, "Did you see that church?"

I said, "Yes."

He said, "Stop right there because that is where the blessings are."

I said, "What?"

He told me that my longtime dream had to be fulfilled. I didn't understand what it meant. The following day, I drove around Kettering, and I saw a church at the traffic light. I heard a voice in me say, "Do you remember that place?" I pulled over my car and looked at the church schedule. At the Saturday night service in January 2009, I went there and worshiped with members of the congregation, and right after service one lady named Debra Heagy took an interest in me. She introduced herself to me and asked me about myself. She took my address. Then one day she came to my home and asked if we need any help. She saw Joyce and my family at the Sunday service. She asked Joyce what had happened to her arm. Joyce replied that she was shot at Gatumba, and that was when the story began.

Debra asked me, "How about a book about your testimonials?" She thought that instead of only people from Gatumba, we would include other places in the Congo where the Banyamulenge live or were from. She then shared the dream of reading 100 testimonials and that to make a difference, we needed to expose the territory to Central Africa.

This *Voice of Central Africa* is the voices of the Banyamulenge people. Hopefully we will be able to bring to trial the individuals responsible for the genocides and help those who are orphans, widows, and victims of HIV/AIDS.

Debra started to help with my nieces' homework, then she asked me what I was thinking. I told her I wished our stories of being victims of discrimination, of the Gatumba genocide, of the Lubumbashi massacre, and of others in DRCongo could be written and read by everyone. Through it, maybe my tribe will find the very much-needed help for the orphans, widows, and people with different diseases caused by war.

As a matter of fact, from 1965 to the present, the Banyamulenge Tutsi tribes have had no peace in the DRCongo. There have been many civil wars against out tribe, and as a result, many innocent people, including children and women, have been killed.

One of the worst massacres took place in the neighboring country of Burundi in the province of Bujumbura in Gatumba, just three miles from the capital city of Bujumbura and only a few miles from DRC/Congo where in less than three hours, 164 of the Banyamulenge tribe were killed and hundreds wounded during the night of August 13 to August 14, 2004, by rebel groups from DRCongo and Burundi. We will never forget them, and we will always give them honor by remembering all of them.

That is why every year here in the United States and Canada, we and others from around the world, wherever Munyamulenge live, have commemoration days on August 13 and 14.

We honor those 300 young students that were killed by their fellow state officers in the Kamina military camp in 1998 and so many other innocent people in different villages in the DRCongo.

The purpose of this book is to educate individuals about the struggles that my people are going through in my country. Subsequently, we can raise money to help orphans, widows, women, victims of rape, and many other sick people who do not have the resources to get well because of the war.

I would like to thank you, Mrs. Debra Heagy, my American Mom, for the unconditional love and support you have shown to help create this book. Thank you, Mr. Rex Heagy, my American Dad, for all the patience, technical support, and guidance. To those individuals who read this book, I hope that you will learn about what happened to the Banyamulenge Tutsi tribe and will resolve to do something: to help someone.

Introduction

The book is written to share to the world about a special tribe in Africa. They are the Banyamulenge tribe of Central Africa. There are more than 400 tribes in the Congo. This particular tribe has gone through more genocides and hardships than an average individual can begin to comprehend. The lives of innocent men, women, elderly people, children, and babies have been exterminated primarily due to their ethnicity. The remaining survivors are scarred with gunshot wounds and infectious diseases. They will struggle with pain and crippling injuries for the rest of their lives. Young women and men have been beaten and raped and have contracted HIV/AIDS from their enemy. They do not own any land, and they are unable to have their own homes. They live in constant fear. They reside in crowded tents where food, water, and medical attention are scarce. Government corruption only compounds their fears for safety.

Two terms used in this book are genocide and massacre. The terms are used interchangeably throughout the content and in the hundred-plus testimonies of the people interviewed. Allow us to briefly define the terms.

Genocide[1]: the deliberate and systematic destruction of a racial, political, or cultural group.

Massacre[2]: the act or an instance of killing a number of helpless of unresisting human beings under circumstances of atrocity or cruelty.

In the following testimonies, the events in the individuals' lives are true. These individual experiences are described in some cases as unpleasant and in others as miraculous. The Banyamulenge people share spiritual, cultural, and historic topics in depth in hopes of gaining understanding from the individuals who read this book.

Who are the Banyamulenge?

With regard to the words "Banyamulenge" and "Munyamulenge," it should be noted that the prefix "mu" refers to the singular and the prefix "ba" to the plural. The Banyamulenge are Congolese Tutsi who live in the South Kivu (a province located in eastern RDC). Originally from Rwanda, Burundi, and Tanzania, they settled in the South Kivu region three centuries ago. Since their arrival in the Congo, the Banyamulenge have been denied their citizenship and rights by Congolese authorities through inciting some Congolese extremists against the Banyamulenge, even though the Banyamulenge have made the Congo their home for four centuries. The government failure to resolve this crucial issue of the Banyamulenge citizenship, and provision of equal rights and treatment for every Congolese, has under-

---

[1] Webster's New College Dictionary, G. & C. Merriam Co., Springfield, MA ©1973

[2] Webster's New College Dictionary, G. & C. Merriam Co., Springfield, MA ©1973

mined regional security and contributed to several perilous situations such as the 1996, 1998, and 2004 killings, atrocities and massacres. It is the government's responsibility to ensure that every one of its citizens enjoys national rights and privileges, one of the keys to ending the current chaos that the country has sunk in for years. (Information courtesy of Olivier Mandevu, President, Gatumba Refugee Survivors Foundation, Inc., http://www.gatumbasurvivors.org.)

In Jolie Uzamukunda's testimony, she mentioned positive attributes of the Banyamulenge people. Most of the Banyamulenge people are Christians, and they always start churches no matter where they go. They have many churches in Rwanda, Burundi, Uganda, Kenya, Europe, and the United States. Uzamukunda stated that they live by the verse in the Bible (Mark 16:15) which says, "As you go into the entire world, proclaim the gospel to everyone." This is what Jesus told his disciples, and it is the reason why many Banyamulenge never stop preaching the gospel wherever they go.

Again, who are the Banyamulenge?

People say that the Banyamulenge originated from Rwanda at the pre-colonial time, when they settled in the high plateau of Itombwe. However, some historians think that they are Nilothics from Burundi (Abongera, Abanyakarama) from Tanzania (Abaha, Abahinda, Abapfurika) who searched for grazing land to join those coming from Rwanda. They settled in Itombwe eventually to form an ethnical group of people called the Banyamulenge.

Where did the name Banyamulenge originate?

First, the name derived from Abanyamulenge, which were the Hamites from ancient times who might have settled in the Great Lake region at the time of the Kingdom of Abanyiginya in the eleventh century.

Second, the name Banyamulenge derived from the Mulenge village.

Depelchin, commenting on an oral history given by Constantin Gasore, clarified by stating: "Continuing their migration to Itombwe High Plateau, the shepherds founded their first village between the Sange and Remera sectors. They created a significant center and called it Murenge. Many years after the village became their capital, they were called this name by their neighbors. The village was created in 1850 to 1860 on the plateau of the Mitumba Mountains, near the overhang of the mountain. They had an administrative organization and were led by traditional chiefs to whom they could pay respect.

"When the white man came they tried to break their solidarity through their leaders, and in 1923 they took one of their famous leaders, Kayira Bigimba, at the high plateau of Itombwe. The white man had the career of purchasing Pygmies and destroying their dwelling places of Carnivorous or flesh-eating animals (ferocious or fierce)."

Regarding the population of Itombweby, the Banyamulenge:

The first man who crossed the Ruzizi River was Serugabika. He might have just crossed the river searching for grazing land in the dry season and so he could bring his livestock to drink water. Then he found the land which was good for grazing and planting. Finally, they decided to live in this place. Later on, he brought his family, and he was followed by some neighbors.

According to the traditional history, the Banyamulenge might have crossed the Ruzizi River to migrate in pre-colonial Congo in 1510 to 1543 at the time of the Garinga Kingdom.

These people are descendants from Byinshi, son of Barama.

According to Alexis Kagame in the Ethno-history of Rwanda, the Banyabyinshi left pre-colonial Rwanda at the death of Yuhi II Gahima in 1444 to 1477.

In Rwanda, this became the time when Ndoli, son of Ndahiro II, was enthroned. He lived at Karagwe and was the man enthroned under the name of Ruganzu II Ndoli (1510-1530). He attacked Byinshi and killed him. The pursuit of Byinshi's sons had become widespread, it is the way of all Byinshi's descendants and supporters. They were obliged to flee and arrived at Ruzizi Plain. They occupied Kakamba, where they met with the descendants of Serugaba and other families which followed to search for pastures.

Another massive migration took place in 1746 to 1802 due to hunger, called Rukungugu. In Ruzizi, the population was going to flee. Due to the endemic diseases they fled and continued up in the region in the mountains. They founded the village of Mulenge in 1850. They lived at Kakamba in Ruzizi for fifteen years, but because of malaria they relocated to the mountains.

(This information is courtesy of Constantin Gasore, who is Bishop of Restoration Church in the Eastern Province of Rwanda.)

Map courtesy of: Coordinator Nehemie Nkunda RDC/
Department of Health in South Kivu 2010

Timeline

Timeline of historical events from the survivors'
testimonials[3]

- 1963-Congo War started by Bidari from the Bapfurero
  Tribe.

- 1964-Ngatongo Infizi County-Village attack-Tribe leaders
  killed plus others-The rebellious chief named Mulele,
  with the support of the local communities neighbor
  to Banyamulenge, attacked and massacred peaceful
  Banyamulenge peasants in various localities with the
  reason given that they were foreign and against the com-
  munist Village-several killed.

- 1965-Mulele Rebellion-Pierre Mulele-President-against
  the Government-The town of Mubuga in South Kivu-the
  village burned to the ground. Two Villages-Kugatongo and
  Kirumba Village-several groups of twenty to 100 killed at
  a time.

- 1966-Two Villages-Babembe and Bibogobogo-500-plus
  Banyamulenge killed

---

[3] Ruramira B. Zebedee. Thank you for your comments to portions of the
Timeline, August 1, 2010.

- 1979-The neighbor communities were opposed to the creation of Bijombo as a legal county-a majority of Banyamulenge. The reason given was, they are foreigners.

- 1982-The Central committee of the Popular movement of the Revolution, party in power at the time in Zaire, refused all the candidatures of Banyamulenge for the legislative elections for the reason that they were foreign and many exactions, slaughters, arrests, and arbitrary detentions were committed.

- 1987-The political power, influenced especially by the politicians of f Kivu area where the Banyamulenge live, had not only decided that Banyamulenge could not be eligible in the legislative elections, but that they could not vote, giving the reason that they were foreign. Slaughters and arrests and arbitrary detentions of several months followed against Banyamulenge.

- 1990-War of Liberation in Rwanda-Tutsi were marginalized-Between 1990 and 1993, the Banyamulenge were victims of several violations of the human rights, and they could not circulate freely in the cities like Uvira, Bukavu, and all the urban centers around the Lake Tanganyika and the Ruzizi River without being stoned, lynched, or killed by other means. During the same time, at the time of the National Conference on the democratization of the national institutions to which all the communities were represented, the Parliament of Transition refused the Banyamulenge who represented their community, giving the reason that they were foreign and must return to Rwanda.

- 1994-Genocide in Rwanda-Rwanda lost one million Tutsi people in 100 days

- 1996-East Democratic Republic of the Congo-Mai Mai-a group of many tribes killed-The Vice-Governor of the Region of Kivu, named Lwabanji, publicly declared in the media that Banyamulenge must be exterminated within a time not exceeding two weeks. Soldiers, militiamen, and peasants of the neighboring communities were attacking Banyamulenge by massacring them without discrimination and in a systematic way. The survivors took refuge in forests, and the luckiest ones joined the adjoining countries like Burundi, Rwanda, and Uganda.

- 1998-Massacre started in Tanganyika-Sub-province known as Kalemie-80 people killed at a time-The war reached the Village of Vyura in Moba County August 1998-300 young students from college were killed by their fellow state officer in the Kamina military camp. Burundi (a tree village which was attacked by government militia Troops). They were Babembe who took refuge in Burundi-It is the same scenario of 1996, and the killers tortured and massacred civil populations and Banyamulenge soldiers everywhere in the country. In all the military units of the country, very few soldiers could escape.

- 2002-Rebels occupy Maima-in City of Uvira-Village of Maheta attacked.

- 2003-There was an armed conflict between certain soldiers and young Banyamulenge against the Army of Congo and Army of Rwanda because they considered that there was a plan of deportation of the Banyamulenge community towards Rwanda or elsewhere and forced to leave their country. * This conflict caused several deaths. Until today (2010), there exist groups armed with Banyamulenge young people who do not believe in the leaving of the plan of deportation and in the will of the Congolese Government to protect Banyamulenge.

- 2004-In May, the military commander of the Tenth Brigade named Budja Mabe and his soldiers attacked the Banyamulenge who lived in the Bukavu and Uvira cities; they massacred and burned their dwellings, and the survivors took refuge in Burundi and Rwanda. May 26th in city of Bukavufor-killing because one military commander from the tribe had refused to take orders from his chief-Students and families were killed in the town of Labotte and Ndenderre-killed by government soldiers in presence of MONUC-the peace keeping force currently in the Congo August 13th and 14th- Gatumba Massacre-166 killed and 200-plus badly injured-In August, those who had taken refuge in Burundi in the Camp of Gatumba under management of the UNHCR of Banyamulenge were coldly massacred. Since then, some did not have any more confidence with their safety in Burundi and had taken refuge especially in Rwanda, Uganda, and Kenya.

- 2009-October-first part of month, 4:00 a.m.-Burundien soldiers and police from Mwaro attack the camp to force refugees to another facility-the refugee survivors were badly beaten-500 Banyamulenge-plus

- 2010-From 2004 to the present, the members of the Banyamulenge community are dispersed: those who could not flee are daily in permanent insecurity and victims of the awful exactions of the soldiers; those who had fled are not out of danger in the countries where they took refuge; the example is those who have been massacred in the Burundi camp of Gatumba. Even immediately now, one announced a death of Banyamulenge students killed by militiamen.

List of Survivors

The List of Survivors from Central Africa
Who Provided the Testimonies

Elias Kanyabitabo
Paul Ndayishimiye
Joyeuse Nambabazi
Nicole Mapendo
Laurent Muvunyi
Beatrice Nyankuml
Evariste Ntabareshya
Nyanduhura Naganza
Ramu Nashimwe
Pastor Dieu donne Kinyamahanga
Pastor Zacharie B. Mashavu
Norbert Rwambaza
Christine Murebwayire
Francoise Nyirabashumba
Egide Ngabonziza
Ildephonse Rujonge
Zirayi Nyanyurira
Pastor Eliazard Mudakikwa
Innocent Birume
Therese Nyamasomo
Doctor Norbert Runyambo
Narira Muzinga

Jeannette Nyadiama
Philip Mukwiye
Antionette Uwimana
Mutoni Mukinanyana
Nigute Kanyabitabo
Emmanuel Mushinzimana
Oscar Nzeyimana
Sofiya Nabigondo
Angelique Nyirankumi
Justin Semahoro Kimenyerwa
Chantal Umutoni
Angelique Ngendo
Esperance Nyanduhura
Alpha Nsanga Bahati
Fred Gasore
Pastor John Bizimana
Cecilia Nyirabigazi
Jeanine Nyakirindo
Jerome Mutuirutsa
Pastor Dieu-dodde Mudage, Mugaju
Prudence Munyakuri Nzigiye
Dollard Mazimano
Jolie Uzamukunda
Alexis R. Mbagariye
Pastor Emmanuel Nkundimana, Mihingana
David Byiringiro
Pappy Amani
Antoine Ndasumbwa
Miriam Nyamusaraba
Alexis Shandata
Francoise Bikundwa
Alexis Mugabo
Chantal Nyiramazaire
Pastor Pierre Nzamu
Pastor Adrien Kajabika

Olivier Munezero
Angelique Nyankamirwa
Mechec Sebatunzi
Iragaba Runezerwa
Feza Nyamutigerwa
Jolie Mirika
Fanny Nabagigi
Daniella Namukobwa
Isaac Gapingi
Joseph Rwibutso
Teti Furaha
Mutesi Nabitanga
Emmanuel Nkumdamahoro Mihingano
Nkomezi Rumenera
Esaie Ndayisaba
Obedi Rutandara Bukuru
Chantal Ngineri
Neziya Nashinwe
Rubin Mazimano
Yvonne Nyampore
Esperance N. Budutira
Pastor Nene Rwenyaguza
Chantal Mutirabura
Tite Nyamushemwa
Rusi Nyiramahoro
Patient Murangwa
Claude Rwaganje
Elizabeth Ngombwa
Issac Sebaganwa
Laurent R. Munyamahoro
Etienne Ngenda Bizimans
Esther Namahoro Bukuru
Paul Mukiza
Innocent Rwiyereka
Charles Rumenge

Aimable Nkundabanntu
Aimee Kinyana
Pastor Moise Sebahizi
Zera Nakanimba
Justin Nsenga, M.S.
Rose Mapendo
Doctor Modeste Kigabo Mbazumutime
Dorcas Nyamukobwa
Choco Amone Kimazi
Jeremiah Mazimano
Roland Runezerwa
Freddy Kaniki

Psalm 91:1-16 (KJV)

[1]He that dwelleth in the secret place of the most High shall abide under the shadow of the Almighty. [2]I will say of the LORD, He is my refuge and my fortress: my God; in him will I trust. [3]Surely he shall deliver thee from the snare of the fowler, and from the noisome pestilence. [4]He shall cover thee with his feathers, and under his wings shalt thou trust: his truth shall be thy shield and buckler. [5]Thou shalt not be afraid for the terror by night; nor for the arrow that flieth by day; [6]Nor for the pestilence that walketh in darkness; nor for the destruction that wasteth at noonday. [7]A thousand shall fall at thy side, and ten thousand at thy right hand; but it shall not come nigh thee. [8]Only with thine eyes shalt thou behold and see the reward of the wicked. [9]Because thou hast made the LORD, which is my refuge, even the most High, thy habitation; [10]There shall no evil befall thee, neither shall any plague come nigh thy dwelling. [11]For he shall give his angels charge over thee, to keep thee in all thy ways. [12]They shall bear thee up in their hands, lest thou dash thy foot against a stone. [13]Thou shalt tread upon the lion and adder: the young

lion and the dragon shalt thou trample under feet. [14]Because he hath set his love upon me, therefore will I deliver him: I will set him on high, because he hath known my name. [15]He shall call upon me, and I will answer him: I will be with him in trouble; I will deliver him, and honor him. [16]With long life will I satisfy him, and show him my salvation.

Testimonies

Name: Elias Kanyabitabo

I now live in Texas. March 19th a group of Congolese refugees left the country to start new lives in the United States. In the next few months 500 survivors went to the United States in Denver, Colorado, Louisville, Kentucky, and San Francisco, California under the resettlement program. I lost my wife and eleven year old daughter when men burned and killed 156 people on a refugee camp at Gatamba on August 13th, 2004.

During that time in August, we had a ramshackle house that was shared with four other families. We had to leave the camp because all camps were subject to danger, death, and destruction. My children have vivid memories of burning tents, and gunfire the night of the attack where 800 residents were staying. They were sleeping at the time of attack. Most of the dead were women and children. All the children have permanent physical scars; one shot in leg, another in the hip, and an eye was shot out with many pain problems. The ones who were among the wounded were mediavaced by the United Nations authorities. Many people were treated in Nairobi.

My family was among the 20,000 Congolese who fled Burundi to escape the extensive fighting in South Kivu Province of the Democratic Republic of the Congo in mid

2004. The resettlement allows special medical care and a safe area to live. These people came with hardly any belongings and we knew nobody in the United State. I have ten children and my second spouse, a 53 year old Kanyabitaro left Burundi capital Bujambura to live in Texas in the town of Abilene "The Friendly Frontier."

Now, we have lived six months "free." Our sponsor met our family in Abilene, Texas. I have obtained vocational training and we are currently learning English while living in the states.

Paul Ndayishimiye

Hi, my name is Paul Ndayishimiye.

I was born in 1997. That time my family was in the African Congo. We had war and we left country. People were killed but, God save some of my family. Three people of my family die: my Father, and two brothers then we move to America for now. I am twelve years old.

Name: Joyeuse Nambabazi

I was born in the Congo in 1994 and there was news of my tribe having problems with the government. There was news of some of my relatives and other members of our tribe being killed. A year after this war we moved from our country to the country named Burundi Bujumbura. When we arrived there the government put us in a refuge camp.

When we got in Bujumbura this was where we had the big problem of the genocide in August 13, 2004. That time in the refuge camp we never had peace. In one night 164 people died, some of us were burned and others wounded. In these people who were wounded, I was one of them, they shot me on my shoulder and killed two of my nieces. After being shot, I fell down with one of my nieces on my back. In the morning people took me to a hospital, after HCR decided to bring us to the United States, to Ohio. Until today, I have had five operations on my right shoulder and arm. In the present time, my hand is still paralyzed because, I'm Christian and in my heart I forgive them. May God bless them.

Name: Nicole Mapendo

This is my story of my past. My name is Nicole Mapendo, I was born on September third

1984 in the Congo. I was born in a large family with five girls and four boys. We live in Congo for many years, but we did not have freedom as native born in that country until today.

In 1998-1999, we had race problems in the Congo. The government decided to put us in one place refugee camp once we were citizens in the country. In Congo, we had many tribes, but our tribe had to be treated with soldiers in charge. We had a tuff moment in Congo. I cannot imagine it until now. People were coming to my house that time I was around thirteen to fourteen, they were beating us, shouting and gossiping us a lot. Then two of my brothers were killed and until today we never had there bodies returned to family. It does hurt my heart to think about my brothers missing. After about fourteen months the people including myself were staying in jail, were taken to USA. Then, my mother claimed us like refugees to come to the USA.

When I came to the United States, I did my high school and some my college, until I decided to get married to Laurent. According to my belief thru my heavenly Lord, I already have forgiven all who had hurt my heart and feelings for many years. The Bible says that in Christian life we need to be forgiven. The forgiveness in our heart and I'm sure I already did with all my heart. That's why I want to help Laurent and Jean who is still back in Rwanda, Africa.

After getting married to Laurent, we decided to move from Maine to Ohio, because we have a plan with God. He sent us here to do his work with helping the orphans, widows, and people who have diseases, crippling war wound injuries, HIV and Aids.

Laurent, his brother Jean, and I started a new project organization called ARDR that will provide assistance people have from disease to war related injuries. We encourage people help in whatever capacity because the Lord says lets help each other through anything as Christ people.

One day Laurent went to attend a Church of God on Marshall Road, and Laurent and I found our church home. The people from this church treat us like we are a part of the family in Christ. May God Bless Pastor Kevin and everyone in the Marshall Road Church of God.

Name: Laurent Muvunyi

My name is Laurent Muvunyi and I was born in the Congo August 10, 1977. Since four generations of our tribe called Banyamulenge Tutsi had problems with the Congo government and other tribes to the present time. In my tribe, we were never treated equally but as a minority to other Congolese.

The government of the Congo and other tribes killed a large portion of our Banyamulenge community to the present time. The Banyamulenge tribe had only one school for all the community which means after high school we do not have the freedom to attend college or a university as other Congolese tribes of the Congo. I remember we did not have a chance to go to different schools, medical schools, science, theology, or schools of the arts. Some people who have a friend in government could attend other colleges but not too often.

The genocide started in 1960 to 1973 with our tribe and many people of our tribe died. Other people of our tribe were held captive, burned and eventually by the militia called Mulele. In my family, one brother, two sisters were taken captive. They were very young when the attack happened at my parents home. Thirty children were playing together and were killed while some were violently burned. But God, prevented harm to my family. My brother and sisters came back from captivity after several years and are still alive today.

In 1980 to 1990, many students went to universities and were killed. In 1993 to 2004 we had many genocide in Likasi, Kalemi, Kinshasa, Lubumbashi and refuge camps in Burundi. We lost many people and at the Burundi Refuge Camp we lost 164 people in one night and 346 total from the attack.

For myself, we left the country and went to Rwanda which also had some problems of genocide but, God protected us. After my high school I went to college for community development and project management for four years bachelors degree. After all the bad times, my brother Jean and I decided to create a nonprofit organization called ARDR to give aid to the people with disease, war injuries, HIV, Aids, orphans and widows. Now we have over five hundred orphans who need our assistance to live. Our office is in Rwanda, but we support Rwanda, Burundi, and the Congo. We need support from people who have the desire in their heart to help God's people.

I met Nicole Mapendo in the Burundi before she left to go to the United States. That time she was very young but we keep our communication by email and sometimes she would call me in Africa. We became engaged when I came to the United States. We planned to have a wedding in July 5, 2008. When I was still in Burundi, I was in college and worked with our mission ARDR. I met Jean Paul when he was in the refugee camp in Burundi. Then after the genocide

2004, I went to Burundi to see the survivors of the attack. I saw Jean Paul was in the hospital with Joyeuse.

From 2003 to 2006 my occupation in ARDR was to work with different churches about orphans and HIV/AIDS program. ARDR stands for the Association Rwandaise Pour le Development Rural. Until now I am the Legal Representative for ARDR in the United States and I'm looking for support from churches and individuals interested in helping my mission with ARDR.

When I came to the United States as a refugee, I went to Maine to stay with my friend Franks. After a few months, I decided to marry Nicole in July of 2008. We decided to take our time to pray what direction the Lord wants us to go. We prayed on where to go and to find people who understand our vision and support for the ministry. God is good. We have Pastor Kevin, Rex and Debbie as well as the church family for support.

Name: Beatrice Nyankuml

August 13th at around 10pm, I was in bed when I heard noise of people yelling and they said, "Today your God left you." I heard shooting in a few minutes and I heard another shot. Pastor Minyati was sleeping next to me in other room and he was dead. I was next and "I lose mind, I was shot." One month gone when my mind came back, I was in hospital, Prince Louis Rwagasore. After I spent one month there I was transferred to Nairobi Hospital. Until that time I lose my right eye. The other people, I don't remember because I was shot in the first group.

I was born in 1989 in the Congo. I was baptized in 1995 and that time I received salvation and change in my life until now. My life after Genocide is very hard because I lost my eye in Genocide in Gatumba. Most of the time, I still have pain. All of my family is together in Texas except my Mom who died in Gatumba. You have my permission to use my testimony and picture in book.

Name: Evariste Ntabareshya

We lived in Rwanda 1990 and APF, "The Army Patriotic Front," was attacked in Rwanda, and that time every Tutsi had problems. In 1993 we started to hear our neighborhood. They came to our homes and said," this is your time to be killed." When night comes, they took parents and went to kill them out of the village. One of my friends called Habimana, they took him and killed him. From that day, my Dad said do not go to school anymore, because if you continue to go to school you will be killed too. We stayed home until 1994, when real Genocide started. One evening we heard that the present Habyarimana died, all the neighborhood people took machetes, guns, and all kinds of metals. They said that we had to kill all Tutsi. In the morning when we left our homes, we got to a roadblock, they took my Father and cross by the machete, they cut him into pieces in our presence. Then they said, they will kill us after, that time they saw another man they ran to him, so we left the place. When we moved forward we met other militias, who killed three brothers. That time they took one woman and did violation to her. Others were thrown in Muhazi Lake. They burned one man called Ruhumuriza and all his family. After they barantema so I lost my mind and that and that time I spend most of time in a small field area. I saw people with uniforms and they asked me to come and to be treated. Hurt severely with a machete on the back area of head and neck area. I was stinky, all the people ran from me then nobody could take care of me at all.

I was born in Rwanda 1975. The District of Buyoga of Buyoga Cellule Bihinga. After being in that situation, I saw one person tell me that there is no other way I could have peace without Jesus. I received Jesus in my life. My

Mother and five of my brothers are in other Province, but all my brothers are handicapped. I am not working because my head is broken. See my picture and I need help in prayer and assistance. You have my permission to use my name and story with picture in the book.

His father's name is Seburibya Thasian, and his mother Mukandutiye Juliene is still alive. The family's one brother and two sisters were killed. There names were Munyampundu Vincent who was the brother, and the two sisters names was Nyiraneza Verona and Niyobyose.

Name: Nyanduhura Naganza

On August 13, 2004, It was night time around 10pm, I heard guns and people said, "kill every Tutsi we do not want to see Munyamulenge again." People said skip we are attacked, but the camp was already surrounded by militias. They started to shoot and burn. That time I had been shot on my hand and legs, I had five children and two of my daughters was killed by militias at the same time.

I was born in the 1968 in Congo Rurambo. I was baptized in 1974 and I was changed "born again." I have some children with me here in South Dakota, but other members of my family are still in refugee camp in Rwanda, Burundi and Kenya where they live in a hard situation.

I do not work now, because my right hand is paralyzed by the gunshot wound from the genocide. My life now is very bad. I spend most of time in the hospital. I had eight surgeries. You have my permission to use my testimony in your book because it is true what happened.

Name: Ramu Nashimwe "Paul's Mother"

On August 13th, 2004, I was in my bed and I heard noises of people crying and they said, "today your God left you." I heard shooting in a few minutes. My husband and two sons ran because they also heard the shooting. That time the militia rounded up everyone and they started to burn people. The government troops tried to stop, but it was too late. I was so scared.

I was born in January 1, 1967, in the DRCongo. I was baptized in 1974 and that time I received Salvation and change in my life to today.

My life after the genocide is very hard. I had six children and I lost my husband and two sons. I lost one of my little sisters who was with us in the shelter was shot very bad on her shoulder. So now I have trouble with my left leg and right hand most of the time. I still have problem with pain.

I am now not living with all of my family because some live in Rwanda and Bujumbura. I give you my permission to use my testimony in your book.

Name: Pastor Dieu donne Kinyamahanga

On August 13th, 2004 at 10pm, I was in my bed and I heard the noise of guns and people shouting. Then after a few minutes we heard many guns and that time they started shooting in our shelter and started cutting people with machetes. In my family, three people were shot. My wife was pregnant and they shot her in the belly, but God protected the baby. After one month, the baby was born and my wife stayed in the hospital for a while due to prolonged illness.

I was born in January 1, 1965, in the Congo. I was baptized in 1983 and I received salvation. My life is changed now.

My life after the genocide was very hard, because three in my family were shot and were all in the hospital. I had to take care of them all till they were recovered. I have five children and not all of my family is together. Some of them live in Rwanda and Bujumbura.

I give you permission to use my testimony in your book. I work at a hospital in Texas and life is very good now. Life would be better if all of my family was together enjoying what I enjoy.

Name: Pastor Zacharie B. Mashavu (Laurent's Father)

My name is Pastor Zacharie B. Mashavu and I was born in the Congo in 1924.

I was on my farm and I heard a voice from where I was and said "to follow me" and I asked, "who are you?" The voice said, "I am God not the goddess, because I am God who heard and spoke." That time I started to pray that God heard and talked to me.

I was baptized in 1952 with Pastor Yuma Ruben. I was married the same year to Elizabeth Ngombwa. My wife was also baptized in 1952, Elizabeth and I kept in prayer and we also were changed. That time my Pastor trusted me and gave me an opportunity to serve the church as a leader. After I started school, as a teacher of an elementary school. In my class I had twenty students, which I remembered some of their names such as Kabirigi Enoc, Musafiri Aaron, Ruhanga Joel, Ntiha Rusty, Sehumbya Rutare, Kukamirwa Tomas, Nzigirwa, Bideri, Rutungisha Laban, Munyaka Yanza, Kabi, Mbangutsi and others. I taught them the first year with the help of one of the missionaries who came named Ruhekanya Jean. That missionary was called Simon Petron from Sueden. I learned how to read and write in 1945 without going to school. Other people had the same vision are still alive and their names were; Nzamu Peter, Mihana Jean, Madabagizi Nanias, Mugunga Isaac, and Pastor Kajabika.

I served God in Rwanda and the Congo. I did not have a salary in all my years I served God.

I went to school to study the Bible in 1958 in a place called Uvira Gasenga. When I arrived there I asked the missionary if I can come to school because I did not have any education. He told me that this was impossible and he gave me a test. I passed the test and I was able to start school with other students. He could not believe how great I was by comparing with the other students who had the same education. I pass through many problems in my evangelism. During this time our community would ignore what we believed of an unknown God. They said we could eat chicken and goat because their goddess called Nyabingi which meant Ryangombe and Binego. "A women figure."

In the Congo, the war started in 1963, and the person who started the war was called Bidari. He was originally from the Bapfurero tribe. We left our place and they killed many of us, that time other people were held captive. Three of my children were among the others held captive. Their names were: Oscar Nzeyimana, Judith Nyirabigogoro, and Angelique Nyirankumi. The others that were held captive with them are Shyurhu Mutotezo and Nyirabijangara. During that time we organized many to pray and ask God what happened? We heard a voice say, "All the people who were held captive will come back home." That time I started praising God and thanking him for his voice. After Four years, all of my three children came back home safe, I could not imagine that situation. I really believe in the power of God.

The servants I knew were killed: Pastor Jean Nyabuhungu, killed with all the church members in a place called Kirumba Village. The survivors were women and children, Pastor Dugari, Pastor Muganwa, Pastor Rwanjari, Chief Mushishi "Head of Tribe," Chief Byambu, and Chief Binono.

I have seen people die and I have become stronger in my faith with God. I have shared my story and many people have been saved. Until now, I still know how to write well and I found a scripture in Psalms 92:15, "They will still bear fruit in old age, they will stay fresh and green, proclaiming, the Lord is upright; he is my rock, and there is no wickedness in him."

After the genocide, I was still committed to serve God. My life changed day by day from 1924 to the present. I am not with all of my family. Some of my children are in the Congo and others are in a refugee camp in Rwanda. My son, Laurent is in the United States, in Ohio. I do not have a job now, and I give you my permission to use my name and story in book.

Name: Norbert Rwambaza and his wife, Nyagicumbi

In 1998, I was in Lubumbashi for a visit. I needed to go in town to buy a cow. That evening, we heard noise and yelling, "Kill! Kill! Kill Tutsis!" from the congolese army. That time they took ten people and put in a car and went to one commander Papa Seven. Once there, we were put in a small jail room. We met eleven other people, then there was twenty-one of us close together. We all were held close together with a cord. We spent one week without food or water in this room.

The second week we were given some food from the Congolese army. He gave small amount to me and I vomited out because we did not have any food for a period of time. In one day at 3pm the militia came inside the room which is a jail and asked us to take all our clothes and underwear off. They brought another man Nehemie into the room. I another hour, they brought his wife to say "goodbye" to all the people, twenty-two total. They were going to kill her. She cried after seeing her husband there. The militia took her and killed her in front of everyone. Her husband left $10,000.00 in his pocket and was trying to tell the militia to take the money and leave them alone and let them live. They spent five more days in the jail. "The Twenty-One."

The commander took the group of twenty-one people out and put in a car to bring them to another army camp named, Rido. This camp is "known to kill" everyone. Once in camp Rido, they took five of the twenty one people to kill and the rest of the seventeen remained alive.

The time President Kabila gave an announcement on radio "If you still have people in jail, do not kill them, because the United Nations said to stop killing people." "Leave alone the people in jail, do not kill anymore!"

The seventeen of us people spent one month without food or water. We prayed to God and he answered our prayer for water. One night we saw water come in the jail and everybody tried to drink as much water as they could. That day water came from the wall "it was a miracle!" We met more people inside jail. Then one night the militia took twenty-three young people out of jail and killed them. The next day everyone was taken out of jail and transferred to a big prison called, Bakita. Once we were there in jail, I met Nicole, later to be Laurent's wife, and her family. The people looked very bad. They had no food or water.

Five Doctors were sent to help the people in jail. The Doctors said to not give the people food or water, they would all die. The Doctor ordered that everyone be given water with sugar in small amounts for three days. After three days, a sauce made with potato was to be given in small amounts to everyone. Afterward, we met three hundred people in jail, men, women, and children. We all started to pray to get out of jail. One person in the jail heard from God that everyone in jail will be alright and saved. "Liberation from God." After nine months in jail, we saw some white people and people from the Congo government come inside to meet everyone. The white people were from the United Nations of New York. The white person said, "I am from New York and I represent the United Nations. I promise that no one will be killed again from now on, because the United States of America gives me permission to come to see you in jail and bring back reports to the United Nations of the United States." One of the people in jail asked "how can we trust that we will not be killed again?" The man from New York said, "to have two people from jail meet in the hotel." I can ask them more questions since most of them cannot understand English. The two people from jail selected was, Muco who is Nicole's Uncle, and Norbert, "me." We went to meet in the hotel and the people from the UN said, "not to worry, you will be safe." From this time forward we had more visitors from the Red Cross come. One white who was a manager for the Red Cross asked them, "I have instruction from the United Nations to try to have countries accept you as refugees. We take some people to Rwanda only if they have a family, but if not they go to refugee camp. Many people go to the refugee camp in Rwanda. Norbert stayed in jail, Nicole's mother, brother, and many people stayed. In one month they went to the United States. The United States said they would accept you to come to the U.S., but you have to be screened and tested for disease before entry. These people before they entered the states went to the African country of Benin for six months.

I was born in the Congo in 1972 in the name of village of Sange. I was baptized in the Congo. I received Jesus as my Savior. My life after genocide is very bad. I went to Benie refugee camp when I came out of jail. Life was very bad. I am separated from my wife, and three daughters, mother father sisters and brothers who are all in the refugee camp in Rwanda. I want so much to have all of my family in the United States.

My job today is I work with Barber Food Company, "chicken food product." I have worked for the company for nine years. My present position is like "Heaven." I have a house, car, and money in the bank. I have an American passport, I also have become a citizen in the states which allows me to travel. I now have my wife and four children. The children attend a nice elementary school. Their names are Nyabega Nyankema, Antoinette Nyamuryango, Nyasafari Nahumure, and the youngest born in the United States who in Moses Kwambaza. I enjoy the United States, now I have everything and you may use my testimony in your book.

Name: Christine Murebwayire

In 1990 when the RPF army started the war of liberation in Rwanda, so many things that I have gone through [starting to weep]. I remember many things that is why you see me weeping and sorry for it. In 1990 all our families were intimidated and put in jails. The Genocide of 1994 is very difficult, but I will tell you briefly. My family was exterminated; my husband, children, and many of my relatives. What makes me furious and sorrowful is the way I was raped and I am now HIV positive. I cannot tell you everything, but it was unimaginable.

I was born in 1969 in Rwamagana District at Kigabiro Sector at Eyanya Sector. I do not live with anyone, my family is all gone. I do not work. I became lame during the genocide. You have my permission to have my testimony and picture in your book.

Name: Francoise Nyirabashumba

In 1990, when the RPF army started the war of liberation in Rwanda, the Tutsi people were marginalized. We fled the area to Nyagatare District of Easter Province. Now, people are traumatized because of what they saw: parents, children, boys and girls, old and young being shot and killed.

The consequences of the 1994 Genocide are so many. I have chronic HIV/AIDS, and no family due to genocide. I have a responsibility for many orphans of my relatives who have died.

I was born in 1959 in the Rwamagana District at Gishali Sector at Bwisange Cell. All of my family is gone and I do not work. You have my permission to use my testimony and picture in your book.

Name: Egide Ngabonziza

In January 1, 1990, when the RPF army started the war of liberation in Rwanda, I faced so many problems. On March 1, 1990, I was coming from Rwamagana to Kigali. When we reached Masaka, it was very dangerous; a barrier of Ex-FAR, [Ex Rwandan Forces] stopped us asking for identities. They asked me to give it to them, I accepted. In identity it was indicated whether you are Hutu, Tutsi, Twa, or naturalized. I gave the identity card to them and it was very hard to escape. They started to beat me bitterly. I remember at noon when we heard a gun shooting at Dereva Hotel many people ran away on the 5th of October, in 1990. I was thirty years old on that day. The people were gathered at my house along with my family, to be all killed. It was terrible! The same day they put us in jail, where eighteen Tutsis were in prison. I was separated from my family, my wife and children forever when the negotiations began. I cannot finish everything, it's just in brief.

I face many consequences after the 1994 Genocide. My children were killed and my home destroyed. The lack of my family and many people who were traumatized. I have a heavy burden of taking care of many orphans, from relatives who were killed, to support.

I was born the 25th of December, 1960, in the Rwamagana District in Munyaga Sector at Muhungu Cell. I do not have family, They were all killed. I work as a farmer. You have my permission to use my testimony and picture in your book.

Name: IIdephonse Rujonge

In 1990, when the RPF army started the war of liberation in Rwanda, I was put in jail. I was accused of collaborating with the RPF. We were a group of Tutsis, being punished for who we were. In prison one of us died because of the bad conditions we are exposed to. Another person was killed. Tutsi people were brought to Sesera where they were easily killed. We went through many horrible events.

The consequences faced from the 1994 Genocide are many. They killed my children and destroyed my home. The Genocide destroyed my family and life. They cut me severally on the neck, and I am HIV positive.

I was born in 1966 in the Rwamagana District at MuhaziSector in the Murambi Cell. My family died in the Genocide. Now, I work as a farmer. You have my permission to use my testimony and picture in your book.

Name: Zirayi Nyanyurira

During August 13th in 2004, it was around 10pm. I was in bed and I heard the noise of guns and people screaming. They said, "there are strangers here!" Then after a few minutes we heard many guns and that time they were shouting in our shelter. Four people were killed in that moment. I saw another shooting where it involved; Marisyana and two grandsons, one young boy, and one lady with a baby. Evangelist Rukamirwa was a burden and at that moment they shot my first daughter, my son, and myself with child in belly. They burned all of our shelters. I found out myself while I was in the hospital.

I was born in January 1, 1971 in the Congo. I was Baptized in 1984 and at that time I received Salvation and change in my life to present time. My life is very hard after the genocide. I had four children that time and I had been shot in my belly while I was pregnant. I spent two months in the hospital and that was a real struggle.

I am not with all of my family. Some of my family live in Rwanda, and others live in Bujumbura. I give you permission to use my testimony in your book. I now work in Texas and life is very good. I want all my family to join in the same life I have now.

Name: Pastor Eliazard Mudakikwa

I'm Eliazard N. Mudakikwa, I was born in Kishembwe, Uvira on April 2, 1958. I am the son of Ndagano and Namberwa, a Congolese national. I am married with seven children including four girls and three boys of which one died. Currently, I have two grandchildren, son and two small girls.

I have a Bachelor's degree in theology with 'Coronation" average in Enseignement Superieur. I was baptized by immersion on 1/4/1971. I received today the transformation of my young age. I was dedicated in the pastoral ministry on March 4, 1981 in the Church of the Assemblies of God of the Congo, specifically in the local church in Minembwe. I was designated as Regional Secretary of the Assemblies of God in Kivu April 1989. It is from March 15, 1991, that I will be elected to lead the local church Kimanga, Uvira j'exerce function as before. The two functions of Provincial Secretary of the Assemblies of God in the Congo at South Kivu and the Head Pastor of the local church were conducted concurrently.

We have experienced periods of unrest and wars, this meant that I had to flee my country more than four times in ten years. Indeed, by September 1996, I escaped death when Kamanyola driven pastors and several colleagues fideles were systematically massacred. As Pastor: Mahota Rukenurwa, Ndatabaye, Sebugorore, Gashindi, Kashaje,

Rukinisha, Yeremie, Yona Gategeko, Adonis, Gasavubu and Reverend Bugunzu, Pastor Semutobo and Muzuzi are assasinated seven months in the case of Refugees in Rwanda, Bugarama. Following a relative calm, I returned to Uvira to continue my work in the church. In August 1998, the Rassemblement Congolais por Democracy {RCD} trigger yet another rebellion which we take our refuge in Burundi for three months. There was resettlement in October 2002, the rebels occupied Maima again in the City of Uvira, while Rwandan contingents support from the RCD had to return home. All the Banyamulenge in Uvira had death threats and we fled to Burundi. The most crucial was the outbreak of the war of 2004. On June 10, 2004, we had to go to the Gatumba Refugee Camp. Two months after on the night of the 13th to the 14th of August 2004 at 10pm, we were surprised by heavy weapons fire. The coalition was wrong to attack. Several people were brutally massacred, men, women, and children as well as older people were killed indiscriminately. The dead and the survivors were burned alive in tents. We lost 164 people that night and there were more than 200 wounded.

Some survivors have been resettled here in the United States of America, Canada and some in Europe. We deplore the fact that many widows and orphans still languishing in poverty in the darkest of refugee camps in Burundi, Rwanda, Uganda and Kenya.

God gave me the opportunity to seek refuge here in the USA but, my family is still in the refugee camp in Burundi. I continue to preach the Good News of the Lord and hope that a door will open and I will be able to rejoice and praise the Lord with my church family as well as the members of my family. May God bless you.

Name: Innocent Birume

This is an unforgettable date in the life of the whole community. This event affected me personally and others who were injured physically for life. The tragic event will never leave my heart. This really had me recall all the killing of the Banyamulenge of Bukavu, Kamanyola and elsewhere in 1996-1998. After the attacks perpetrated, by the groups arm to the camps of the Congolese refugees of Banyamulenge of Gatumba in the night of 13th August, 2004, 166 casualties have a record on the place of which 90% vicinity constituted women and children. This mass murder inflicted on this population is a consequence of the blows of bullets, automatic guns, other weapons of destruction along with burns engraved with carbonization. The injured victims from these vicious attacks are; 122 cases constitute 17 men, 48 women and girls of age 18, 65 children from 4 weeks old to 18 years of age. These victims who were injured and required medical care from the city of Bujumbura as well as other physical challenges are as follows: I had not any means of transportation and communication to do all the races of surveillance, restoration of the patient's health, problems of transportation of some injured to other healthcare facilities outside of Buja. Injured people who were severely wounded physically and mentally were affected by the NGO that were responsible. Problems of disease and infection added to the principal diagnosis [injuries] affected me when I arrived to hear the crying of the injured in front of the sanitary authority of certain institutions. But with God, we will overcome this moment in our life and move on. In Rwanda, it will take more than money to rebuild, and the representative's speech of the Rwandan Government to condemn these behaviors of the persons in charge of the slaughters or genocide. The Congolese and his government were telling us it was a mission organized by the high Congolese authorities. I have received the message of the moment through Prophet Branham I have again been baptized in the name of Jesus Christ, December 6, 1986. Today I am a convinced Christian, that Jesus is the only God. Now, we have a family of nine children, and we are all to the WORE, but my Dad is at the Rwanda with a statue of the refugee. I am not working and I do not have any problems at the present time. Important events and certain engagements are my only responsibility.

Name: Therese Nyamasomo

We left our country many times because we had very bad political issues from 1960 until now. We still have problems as Tutsi in the Congo. On August 13th, 2004, at night around 10pm, I heard guns and people say, "kill every Tutsi, we do not want to see Munyamulenge again." My husband when he heard a noise from the militia, he woke up and said for everyone to wake up, we are being attacked. When he said that, he was shot with his son and his daughter.

I was born in the Congo in 1939 at Mitamba. I was baptized in 1950 and was changed and born again. My family is not all together here in New York. Other members of my family are still in a refugee camp in Rwanda and Burundi. They still have hard times in the camp.

I do not work now. You have my permission to use my testimony in your book, because it is true and it did happen.

Name: Doctor Norbert Runyambo

The war began in 1996 at the East Democratic Republic of the Congo, I fled first in Burundi for four months, then after to Rwanda in 1998. In 1999, we came back home because the situation in the region became a little normal, but it was still too early for us to live in peace because on May 26, 2004, war started again in the city of Bukavofor an unknown reason. As civilians, we had to hide while heavy weapons were being heard everywhere. On May 27, 2004, we were surprised when government soldiers begun killing Banyamulenge again by the simple fact that one of the military commanders from our tribe had refused to take orders from his chief. The first executions of civilians Banyamulenge began at 10am of the same day. Students and families from our tribe were killed in the town of Labotte and Ndendere by government soldiers in the presence of MONUC, the peacekeeping force currently in the Congo.

Among 17 victims, some were patients found in the General Hospital of Bukavu. 36 wounded were later taken care by Cyangugu Hospital in Rwanda, but some of them died. Among these casualties included young girls and women who were raped.

More than 5000 Banyamulenge who escaped to Rwanda and Burundi and left all their properties behind. These were entirely destroyed. Our people who went in Burundi were placed into Gatumba refugee camp where 165 of them were again massacred in the night of August 13, 2004. During this attack children, women, men, elderly were all burned alive under the UNHCR tents. 116 others were seriously injured, and most of them are still hospitalized in Burundi and Rwanda.

I was born in August 23, 1949. I was baptized in 1964. As a young Christian, I belonged to a loving family who fed us the word of God. I was blessed during my study and in my career. Only after 40 years later I understood that God has a plan for my family. I can realize how Jesus loves me because he saved me seven times from physical death and now he gives me eternal life. So you can understand that I grown slowly in my faith. You have my permission to use my name and testimony in your book.

Now, I volunteer into ALI [Abundant Life Institute] to help immigrant people to integrate in the community. I work as DSP [Direct Support Personnel].

I worked as a physician for 28 years. I volunteer in refugee camps in 1996 and in 2004 for three years.

Name: Narira Muzinga

I was in Lubumbashi for a visit in the Congo in 1998. Then, one day we heard the people saying "kill every Munyamulenge" and the situation came to be very bad at that time. I remembered in a few hours the militia started to kill, I saw for myself 104 were killed in front of me. I still remember them all and they were the Banyamulenge Tutsi. They shouted, other militia use machete to kill those people.

I was born in January 1, 1960 in the Congo. I was baptized in 1978 and that time I received salvation and change in my life. My life after the genocide has been very hard. I spent one year in jail and I was separated from my wife and kids. I have five children and I am not with all my family. Some of them are in Rwanda, and Bujumbura. You have my permission to use my testimony in your book. I am currently working in house keeping in Texas and life is very good now. I own my house and all my children are in school. I would like to have all my family come and enjoy life with me.

Name: Jeannette Nyadiama

On August 13th, 2004, it was 10pm when I heard noise of my people singing and saying "today is day for you guy." That time we heard guns and saw fire burning our shelters. Then, my two sisters were shot and killed. In a few minutes they shot my Mom, and we started to run and many people were being burned. The day after that it was a hard time for me to stay with children because my Mom was in the

Hospital. Until now, I still have responsibilities to take care of my young sisters and brother, my Mom is paralyzed in her hand.

I was born in 1990, in the Congo. I was baptized in the Burindi Refugee Camp in 2006 and that time I received Jesus as my savior. When we came to the United States, we left some of our family in Bujumbura Refugee Camp.

I work part time because I am a student in high school in South Dakota. My life after the genocide in Gatumba was very bad. My Mom was shot and she spent most of her time in the hospital. You have my permission to use my testimony in your book.

Name: Philip Mukwiye

I was born in 1958 in a town of Uvira. I have sixteen members of my family. Two wives live currently in Kentucky. I lost two sons and one sister, one nephew, and two nieces the same night at Gatumba. I want to bring all of my family home, but some of the members in my family are still in Burundi Refugee Camp called Mwaro.

The date August 13th 2004, I was outside the camp for a barbeque. I came later to my shelter, then my sister told me," I think your second wife looks like she is going to deliver and if possible you can go see her." I did not talk too much longer then I went to see her. When I came there, she to me is fine. Maybe the sickness, I may not deliver today. After thirty minutes, I decided to go back in my shelter. Once I go outside, I heard a voice that said, "kill him, shoot him." They used another language different than mine. The Mulashe responded in the same language, "No, I am in your tribe." That time I heard the three different languages which was Kirundi, Kifurero, and Kinyanwanda which means the Militia spoke another language to confuse people in the camp. Then that time he went to the little forest and the shooting of big guns started in the camp. The fire! people were crying and some were being burned alive! Then, in about an hour the whole camp was destroyed by fire. Then, the Burundi police heard this tragedy and came at once, then the militia went away. The Burundi police tried to save some of the victims. I, Philipe came out of the forest when the police came and told what happened. I, Philipe witnessed the whole horrible event.

The day will never be forgotten. If possible, some people survived the event and could be sent to a medical center for treatment.

Name: Antionette Uwimana

I was born in 1965 in the Congo, the place called Ruzizi. I was baptized in 1979 in South Kivu. I had five children, two were killed in Gatamba, along with my husband in August 13, 2004. One of my children was injured in the right hip. We now live in Columbus, Missouri.

In Gatamba, at 10pm August 13, 2004, my husband and brother went downtown to Bujumbura for the day. When they came back to the refugee camp it was 8pm. They shared the news of their day with the other families who lived in the shelter. After spending two hours together we heard songs and people yelling out loud "today, is your day to be killed, and exterminated." They were using different language to confuse the people at the shelter. Some of the music sounded like Christian music to confuse everybody as well as the army and police. The whole camp was hearing Christian music and thinking all was fine and this was exactly what the militia wanted to do with the people. During that time, the militia saw some people awake and said, "let's kill them!" That moment, the militia came into the shelter and shot my husband, daughter, and brother. All in the first round, they killed members of my family. After that, they shot Gasosi, his wife, and three children. They killed Zaroti's wife, and two children, Michel's wife and child, Pastor Rutekeza and his six children along with Biguge and their two sons. After that, some people were wounded and the militia burned them while they were alive and they died. They poured gas and set fire to the shelter. My son was still alive after being badly burned and he lived for six hours and died.

I still have many family members in the refugee camps in Burundi and Rwanda. They are struggling to stay alive.

You have my permission to use my testimony in your book. Please, if possible, can you help try to bring them home here in Missouri.

Name: Mutoni Mukinanyana

My name is Mutoni Mukinanyana and I will never forget August 13th, 2004 in Gatumba. I have been separated from my family and especially the one that has raised me when I was a child. I have lost all my friends and it has been very hard living without my Mother and sisters.

I was born in the Congo in 1988. I was baptized in July 22, 2001 in Burundi. The time I accepted Jesus as my Lord and Savior.

When I came to the United States, some of my family were left behind in Bujumbura Refugee Camp. I am a student in high school currently working part time in Portland, Maine. I really need to be with my family. It is really hard for me to live as a young girl in this country by myself. My prayer is to be one day reunited with my family. I trust God will give me the chance to see my family one more time. "What I know is God is able." You can use my story in your book.

Name: Nigute Kanyabitabo in Texas

The day in August 13th, 2004 at Gatumba has changed my life. I have been separated from all my family, especially the one that raised me when I was a child. Beside that, I lost all my friends which is not easy for me to live without a parent, my best Mom who in the world the one I can tell all my problems! The one who can try to help me make a decision! I think about my Dad, who always wants to be in a good position! Going to school without any problem! All my sisters! August 13th, 2004 is the day that I am not going to forget.

I was born on December 30th, 1988 in RDC. I was baptized in July 22, 2001 in Burundi, in a Pentecostal Church. My life has changed and the knowledge that Jesus Christ is my Savior.

My family is not all together. Some of them are in Burundi, especially for a student who is trying to get an education. It is not easy for my family who is still in the refugee camp. They do not have any food to eat! They do not have any clothes to wear! The rest of my family are in Rwanda.

I am a student in high school and I have a part time job. You have my permission to use my name and story in your book. You are aloud to use my name any time as long as you are trying to help me in the time of need. The time that I look around to see where my help does come from!

If at all possible I really need to be with my family. My parents are still in a bad situation and it is very dangerous in their life. In all of my prayers and all of my wishes and all of my dreams, I really hope that God is going to give me a chance to see my parents once more. Through God, I know anything's possible.

Name: Emmanuel Mushinzimana

Before the genocide in Rowanda 1994, my family has six children and my parents. That time around April 1994 the situation was very bad for all Tutsi's families. The government was in power and they said, "every Tutsi be killed!" My Father, Mother, and three brothers were killed at our home in the small village. After the genocide, it was hard to stay with other children without my parents.

I was born in 1980, in Rowanda in the southern part called Cyangugu Province. I was baptized in Rowanda, December 20, 2002, the time I received Jesus as my Savior.

I have two sisters that are married and I take care of presently. I work as a driver in Kigali city. I still need some help to go back to schools to take care of my younger sister. You have my permission to use my name and story in your book.

Name: Oscar Nzeyimana

In the year 1965 we had a war called Mulele which was the rebellion against the government. Pierre Mulele was the President of that group and they had to attack all the towns, or villages. My parents live to the south of Kivu in the congo, they were breeders of cows.

In that time of the 1960's, my family had three children which were two girls and one boy. One morning December 4, 1965 in the town of Mubuga in South Kivu, our village was under attack by the rebel with the objective to kill the whole population in this village. The village burned to the ground.

In this time, I was six years old and my big sister was ten years old, and my youngest was four years old. This rebel had guns, machetes and launches. In that day many people were killed and others were held captive. Most of the rebels were children. Among the fourteen children who was held captive, twelve were girls and two were boys.

The distance that we had to walk on foot was fifteen days. The children are beginning to get tired. After they arrive, the place where the militia lived, we were divided in different families. Me, I go to a commander of the Militia, named Poroto. In the first time he took me like a child and after one year, I begin to work as a slave.

The difficult work was to go on hunts and kill lions, buffalo, and elephants. I had to dig a hole of four meters in depth and put grass on top as a trap for hunting these animals. I had to use a heavy gun, and it was hard to use because I was only seven years old, and I also was still treated as a slave. I had to be bound to a tree in order to use the heavy gun to kill animals. I did not have the same position as others. They used me to work hard until my shoulder was broken. Where I was, I was in the big forest. Sometimes the commander of the militia would give an order to see the sun for three hours and then come back into the forest. I did not have much time to see the sun because I was held captive. If I go too far I will run and bring along my two sisters. The militia attacked the village when they captured a village, people were killed. When the militia come back the children were to be tortured and beaten. When they come again they would attack and torture the parents. The children and anyone else would be the slaves. We would spend four years in captivity and work as slaves. I had experience in killing animals. One day the commander gave me an order and he told me to, "go kill animals yourself." He gave me a gun. That time I remember my family. I started to run and it was a long distance for me when I came out of the forest. I see some people who were behind the cows. They saw me and said "who are you?" They were afraid of another militia who was going to attack. I already forgot my native language. I spoke in Swahili "is me," then, I put the gun down. They came and approached me and asked me the name of my parents. I gave the name of my father. The people asked me, "can you show me where you put the gun." I said, "ok, do you remember fourteen children who was captive in 1965?" They said, "yes." "I am one of them." They looked toward the big village and sent a leader for my parents and they came. They brought thirty parents together and they asked me, "do you know your father?" I run and touched my Dad's hand in the group. Many of the people were crying with joy and sadness. Other children were killed and the leader was very happy for my family and other families in the village.

I was born in April 7, 1962. I was baptized in 1979. If you need me to give a testimony in the United States, I will come. I work at a Reconciliation Center in Rwanda. You can use my testimony in your book.

Name: Sofiya Nabigondo

I was born January 1, 1955 in the Congo. I have ten children. Two of my boys were killed in the Congo RDC. We lived in Lumbumbashi, known as the capital of Gatuba. In 1998 we heard on a radio that the RDC were coming. We think the war involved everyone, but in a few days we knew it was against our tribe. Five days the RDC came in my house because my husband was out in the city to do business. They asked me where is your husband and I told them he was out. They took people out of the house, one of my brother in laws was with us. They took him, and beat him, he was the first man to go to jail. Then, me and my eight children were taken to jail. The prison was named "Gene." We spent one month and afterward they transferred us to a bigger jail named "Bakita." We spent fourteen months in this jail, with the suffering, no medicine, no food, no water, no freedom to go outside. We were treated like slaves in jail. I remember we used to have a big farm of about three hundred cows, chickens, sheep, and all were killed along with my two sons. In same jail, my daughter delivered a son. She had difficulty in her delivery of the baby due to the conditions. My problem is I have a daughter and her family still in a refugee camp in Kenya. My wish is they come here and join our family. You can use my story in your book and it is all true.

Name: Angelique Nyirankumi

First of all I have to thank my God for everything he has done for me and all my family. Since 1965, until now, every time a death comes to me and God protected me. In 1965, I was four years old. I didn't know too much except my family, sister and brother. One morning we were outside playing with other children and we heard gun shooting in the village. The village was under attack, and all the children I played with were held captive, including myself, one sister, and one brother was one of the groups that were captive that day. The militia took us captive for four years and we traveled many miles to buy food. My sister was ten years old riding piggyback on my back when the militia came and took us captive. We spent four years in the forest under control of the militia. Children died at that time by disease, hunger, and being beat by the militia. We had a terrible life. I do not know how to explain to people but, everybody can understand how the children could be treated like slaves for five years!!! My God did not leave us alone. We come back, me, my sister, and brother after being held in captivity. I have to thank our parents. They did not give up praying, or hope in seeing us again safely back home with our family. I need to thank the families who lost children still had hope that one day there will be peace.

In 2002 I was married living in one village called "Maheta." We were attacked again and I thought that this is my last day to live. I slept but was not prepared to die in

1996 when I heard again the militia gunfire. My heart said, "do you want to be held captive again?" Before the people left to go home I prayed that God would not leave me or my family. We ran to my house and it was burned down along with our cow that was killed. The same day many of the people in the village were beaten and burned alive. Many people died. Now, I am married, I have eight children, four boys, and four girls. My husband and our family still live in a refugee camp in Rwanda. My life is very hard and difficult.

I have to thank God and the group who decided to take our stories and put in a book. This will let many people know about the difficult moments that have happened to me and other people.

I am very proud today to see my children and parents still alive to see their grandchildren. It is like a dream or vision for my parents to have grandchildren because all three children were held captive, but now we have a huge family. For me, I am very humble in waiting to see this book, whether I know English, or not. I can't wait to see this book and how the people will respond to what we have gone through in our lifetime.

Name: Justin Semahoro Kimenyerwa

I am a Congolese refugee who was resettled in the United States in June of 2009. I would like to tell you about my home and my people. I was born in Minembwe in the Democratic Republic of Congo - over the mountains of the land, deep within the green fields of South Kivu. It is a land full of green vegetation, lush forests, and beautiful wildlife. Between the greenery, numerous rivers always flow among the mountains and flat land. We have two seasons; the rainy season and the sunny season, both marked by favorable temperatures. Throughout the year, a nice breeze offers comfort each morning. Within this peaceful land, there exists a community that struggles to survive. These are the members of the Banyamulenge tribe, they are my people.

The Banyamulenge have lived on the lands of South Kivu for five centuries. It is the home of our grandfathers, our ancestors- the only home we know, but one that is not acknowledged by our neighbors or our government. They believe we have no right to live in the Congo, constantly insisting that we return to our "real" home far from the lands of South Kivu. The unprovoked hatred of the Banyamulenge people has been the cause of indescribable suffering and massive killings of my people.

In 1996 war began in the Congo- a war which continues to this day and one in which a malicious group called the Mai Mai seeks to eliminate the entire Banyamulenge Tutsi tribe. The Mai Mai is a group of many tribes in the South Kivu region (Abafurero, Ababembe, Abanyintu, Abashi, Abarega) that joined together with Interahamwe (Hutu's who fled from Rwanda after they carried out Rwandan Tutsi Genocide in 1994). Together, they started attacking Banyamulenge villages- killing men, women, and children, taking our cattle and burning our homes. While they attacked our villages, those Banyamulenge who lived in other areas of Congo were captured, jailed, and in some cases, killed. My brother, Bizimana Mavugo, was one such Banyamulenge- he was arrested in the town of Kalemie and was killed by machete along with eighty-one others. They were buried together in a single grave. In 1998, my own village was attacked. I remember the sound- shouts, the intensifying beating of drums, guns firing at those who tried to escape. Suddenly, the sound of my father's voice: telling us to run, to each fend for our own life. There was no time to say goodbye.

I ran through the bullets, past the attackers who were shooting us, toward the forest we call Nyarubari. I thank God I was not shot. In the forest, I stood with my cousin, Bogabu, waiting in the darkness for the silence that would signal the end of the attack. I was content to wait there, alive. But, Bogabu was less patient. After sitting in silence for several hours, he insisted on walking out to see if the attackers had left. I pleaded with him to stay put, but he was older and he insisted. As soon as he emerged from the bush he was shot. He cried out to me, But I could not help him for fear of being killed myself. After my cousin was killed, I didn't know what to do or where to go. I remained in the bush alone, confused, waiting to be discovered and slaughtered like the others. But God protected me from the attackers and they did not come to the bush in which I hid in a bush that was surely shaking from the twitching of my nerves.

My life changed that night. It was the last time I saw my home in the green fields of South Kivu. I lost five of my best friends that night, friends with whom I did everything throughout my childhood. I loved them very much. It was also the last time that I saw my parents and my siblings- my father's command to run the last I have heard of his voice. There is no way that I can explain to you in words the troubles that I endured after that night. I have no words to tell you of the hunger I felt from having nothing to eat as I walked through the forest. I survived off the leaves and roots of trees. If I discovered a piece of fruit on the forest floor, it was indeed a good day. Nor can I explain to you the pain that I felt in my heart- the longing I felt for my family and my friends, the desire to run home. Of course, I could not return home and so I moved through the forest- comforted by the protection of God's great trees. I went to a town called Uvira. There were other Banyamulenge in Uvira and I thought I would be safe there. A group of children I encountered upon my arrival in the village, proved this thinking incorrect. "What are you doing here?" They asked, already moving toward me with machetes. "Do you think this is your motherland?" Even young children are trained to hate the Banyamulenge. I decided that it is better to be killed running than to stand still and wait for death. And so again, I ran. It was not until after I escaped that I realized I had been struck in the leg by a machete that been thrown at me. I was lucky. Other Banyamulenge who had approached Uvira, suffered a much worse fate; their bodies hacked apart while they were still alive or burned- simply because we are Banyamulenge and they do not want us in their country.

From Uvira, I journeyed into Rwanda, which was not safe either. In Rwanda, I heard that there was a city in Kenya called Nairobi where I would be safe. I heard that Nairobi was a silent city- a place where I would not hear guns, where I would not hear the cry of women and children who screamed out as they were killed. I decided to go there. I remained in Nairobi for five years. During that time I grew sick of my own struggle. I wished I had someone with whom I could share my days, but I was alone. I had a terrible infection in my sinus that kept me up at night. I missed my parents and my siblings. I missed my friends and our cattle back home. Each day I prayed to God, asking Him to bring me to a place where I could be in peace. I thank the creator of Heavens and Earth who heard my prayer and sent his servant to come and save me.

Of course, I speak of Sasha Chanoff and the organization he founded. Tirelessly, they worked beyond what was asked of them for me and my people. Rose Mapendo found someone to pay for the operation I desperately needed on my sinus- allowing me to breath and sleep for the first time in five years. They helped me find shelter and helped me through the long and difficult resettlement process. And so it is that suddenly, after ten long years during which I traveled the forests of Africa, I find myself in St. Louis, Missouri.

For the first time feeling safe. I still miss my home very much. I still miss my loved ones- my family who I have not seen in ten years. I thank God for I recently learned that one of my brothers and one of my sisters are alive with their families. They now live in the silent city of Nairobi, hoping that one day God will find a way for them to join me here in St. Louis. So that we might live again as a family.

I thank God for keeping me alive and now, allowing my voice to be heard- allowing me to speak on behalf of my Banyamulenge people who have no one else to speak for them. We Banyamulenge, do not have a place to call home. We are hated in our country, our people are displaced across neighboring countries and our attackers follow us- killing us wherever we seek shelter. Many of you may have heard of the massacre of the Banyamulenge at the Gatumba Refugee Camp in Burundi in 2004- a nightmare in which hundreds of men, women and children were slaughtered simply because of who they were. Banyamulenge.

As I said, my whole life changed that night in 1998 when the Mai Mai came to my village. Sometimes I wonder what it might have been to live in my home in peace- among family and friends, tending to our cattle and worshipping the Lord. Strangely, I find that the more I dream the more I remember my old village- the more I believe. It remains a mystery to me how I survived the oppression and suffering I faced during the last twelve years of my life. But, whether I understand it or not, I must accept both that I did survive and that there are others who continue to suffer as I once did.

To those out there who are struggling through a situation they feel unable to overcome, I encourage you to continue to move through your own forest- there is nothing in this life that is permanent. Your struggles too shall pass one day. And for those who have been fortunate enough not to suffer in this life, I ask you to consider my people and others that struggle around the world think of them and consider how you might help.

My remaining wish aside from that of one day being reunited with my family- is that no other child shall cross the difficult path I passed through. I will dedicate my life to working toward that goal. I must once again thank the good people at Mapendo International and my new brothers and sisters at the New City Fellowship in St. Louis. I thank them for welcoming me to their country and for caring for me as my family once did. Everywhere my voice is heard, I will thank God for keeping me alive, I will thank Mapendo, and I will thank the New City Fellowship. You can use my story in your book.

Name: Chantal Umutoni

The day that changed my life was August 13th, 2004, I have been separated from all of my family. The family that raised me when I was a child. Beside that, I lost my friends which is not easy for me to live without these personal relationships. Living without my Mom, my best Mom, who in the world is the one I can tell all my problems! The one who can try to help me make decisions! I think about my Dad who wants to always be in a good position! Going to school without any problems. All my sisters! August 13th is the day I will never forget.

I was born on December 30th, 1988, in R.D.C. I was baptized in July 22nd, 2001 in Burundi in the church called Pentecost Church. This is when my life changed and knowing that Jesus Christ is my Savior.

My family is not together. Some of them are in Burundi which is hard being a student trying to get an education. It is not easy for them who are in a refugee camp and have nothing to eat! The rest of my family are in Rwanda.

I am a student in high school and I have a part time job. You are aloud to use my name and story in your book. If it is possible, I really need to be with my family. I know they are in a very dangerous situation in their life. In my prayer, I really hope that God is going to give me one chance to see my family one more time.

Name: Angelique Ngendo

I was born January 5, 1987 in the Congo. I was baptized October 1998 and I was happy for change in my life.

I was in the Burundi Refugee Camp for three months. I was shot in my back in Genocide which was very hard for me. I had Burundi medical care for one month in hospital. In April 2007, while I was in Missouri, my sister, brother, cousin and Dad, as well as another brother and sister were killed. My Mother is in Missouri with me. I work as a Hotel Housekeeper and make good wages. My injury does not affect work. God helped us thru this, especially the people left in my family.

Name: Esperance Nyanduhura

I was born December 22, 1985 in the Congo. I was baptized December 1986. I was at Burundi Refugee Camp in Gatumba where people were killed. I lost two brothers, a cousin and an aunt, they were all killed. There is six of us left, five girls, one boy and my Mom and Dad. Hopefully, I will get a chance to see them. For my sister and other people who were shot that day, August 13th, on Friday at 10 pm, till 12 midnight, all the killing was finished. They made a fire. My brother who was fourteen, was shot along with my aunt and little brother, were thrown in the fire. They burned from the waist down. They died in hospital.

My Mom came March 13, 2007 to the States. I came April 24, 2007 by myself. I have peace from all that happened. My Lord gave me peace. I forgive them. I work at the Swift Company, where I cut meats. I work from 7am to 3:30pm. In 2005, I finished high school. I was not able to go to college in refugee camp. Our diet in camp was rice, beans and corn. I carried water from a stream in fear of getting hurt. Here in the United States, I have no fear of people.

Name: Alpha Nsanga Bahati

I was born June 6, 1968 in the Congo. I was baptized September 1980 in the Congo. I was in a group being hurt on August 12th and 13th, but I was not shot. I was very scared of what was going on. I was separated from my wife and two children in 1988. My wife's name is Muntamuriza Murekatete. My children's names are Rusamarirkia and Nyirabagorora. Life has not been good, darkness, many problems being separated from family. I have been here in the states for seven months and one day. It has been nine years separation from family. Not knowing anything about my family has been very hard.

I was in jail for nine months two weeks in Zambia. (Big Jail) I had no papers. I left the Congo, skipped Burundi, to Zambia. People were killed but, I was spared.

I go to school in Louisville, Kentucky, learning English. I am sponsored with a nonprofit organization. My rent is paid. I helped the teacher in the Congo for one year and started business. I left my house and farm and moved to the big city. I have an Elementary School education and am in good health. I have gone four days without eating and have dealt with high nineties temperature days.

My family is in Burundi Camp. I am not sure but, think they are there. In one year I am applying for green card.

Name: Fred Gasore

In 2004, around 9pm, I heard guns and people said," kill every Tutsi, we do not want to see Munyamulenge again!" People were being attacked in their local village, surrounded by militia. They started to shoot and burn. That time I was shot in my hand and legs. I was with family. I saw some people killed by fire.

I was born in 1984 in South Kivu of Congo. I was baptized in 1998. That time I was changed and born again. My family are in refugee camp in Burundi, Kenya.

I do not have work now. My life after genocide was very bad. Since the war started, I have never been home. I have been in refugee camp all my life. You can use my testimony in your book, because it is true and it happened to me.

Name: Pastor John Bizimana

I am from the Congo. I was born December 12, 1958. I was baptized June 1972. I changed after baptism. I taught bible study to young children. I taught young people, boys, to do one of three listed: to be a teacher, to go into military, or do business with cows. I decided to do business to sell cows. After I buy cows to sell a large number (6), I spent my family money on the cows. The whole family, once I was given money, I had no cows. After that happened, that night, I sleep, I think to do business with cows was lost. I had a dream that night. I saw one man in 1980, and he said, "I want to choose best way for you." In this vision or dream, I saw the man had a bulletin with various verses written on this paper, on the front and back. Another to choose from was money. Ten in Congo money is like $100.00 in United States value. Highest money in Congo is ten. To choose bulletin with varius verses or take money and put inside bulletin. Money is important to me than a piece of paper (bulletin). The man stated, "No, money is not important but, bulletin with verses is more important." The man stated, "I choose you to be my servant and travel various places in my country and abroad to share and preach my faith." All in my dream, my vision of faith. From that day I decided to go to Christian college for three years. I took two additional years in University Bible College. After graduation, I became Pastor. After visit with man in vision, I received "calling" to become Pastor. That night I became Pastor in my country and abroad.

Life after genocide, I was changed. many people were wounded, killed, and some sent to a neighboring town hospital. Outside the hospital, everything is gone after genocide, "very bad situation."

My family has six children, and six orphans, who lost their parents. I am registered as a refugee. I live outside camp, my mother is in refugee camp. My younger brother died and left two children. The children are in my home. I obtain food from camp because I am registered. I as a Pastor asked permission to live outside camp so I can Pastor to people in or out of the refugee camp. I live in a very small house about the size of Laurent's two bedroom apartment. My house has four rooms and no bathroom, which is outside.

My wife is Zera Nahoza. She was born in 1965. Her health is fine, but since I have been gone for visit in the states, my wife has malaria. They have a clinic where we can get medicine.

The refugee camp does not have any work jobs. I work as a Pastor helping people with problems in the camp. There is nothing to do. I do have church service on Thursday, Saturday, and Sunday. I have several groups, youth and women's program. I have no money to train people. It makes it hard to reach people without use of funds. In the city, there is a large problem of alcohol abuse. People are depressed, no job, no money, and a drug problem. Marijuana is the main drug problem. It can be grown easily and there is an abundance of this grown.

There is a need for funds. This includes: helping orphans, young children with schooling, clothing and to help widows to do a small business. We do not have a church building. We have our church service outside. Our church was destroyed in the war.

The people believed in different ways before they found Jesus. After being baptized, the people have to obey the ten commandments, and believe the one faith. People were baptized in the river. Weather can be a problem in certain rain months due to not having a church building.

We have two seasons. Summer is four months long. Summer starts the end of May to the end of September. We have a rainy season. We have no land, no money to plant crops. For years people did nothing, there is no access to clean water. The people drink water from the river. We do not boil water. There is a lot of illness due to no sanitation. The public toilet is the forest area which can be dangerous at times. In housing, there is no electricity, usually a tent, where people sleep on a mat.

The war started in 1995 and has not stopped. People started to leave. In 1998, the war escalated with more deaths and health related problems. In 2000, various areas where genocide has killed large numbers of people. In 2004 genocide at Gatumba, large numbers of people from the Banyamulenge Tribe were killed and severely wounded. The war is still going on and there are areas that are still very dangerous today.

In closing, you have my permission to use my testimony in your book.

Name: Cecilia Nyirabigazi

I was born in the Congo in 1961, Minembwe, Congo. I was baptized when I was 13. I was Catholic and many people in my village were Christian. It was hard to find a husband if you were Catholic. I decided to be baptized, I was immersed in water. After I was baptized, I felt changed.

Some of my family is still in the Refuge camp in Burundi. My younger son and older son are still in the refuge camp.

My brother was killed on the 13th which left two of his children who are now orphans. They are also left behind.

August 13th at night around 10pm, the family meets together to pray together before going to bed. After that I went outside the shelter and when I come back in, I heard people singing. The shooting started the same time. My brother was shot and I was also shot at that time. I heard one girl behind me say, "they shot me too." Then when her Mom was shot, she tried to see and saw the injury in stomach and leg. That time I lose my consciousness. I woke up in hospital two days after massacre.

I do not work, I am not able to stand two hours. I still have problem with my leg. I am here with my husband and six children. My life is very changed, because I come here in United States to find hospital and Doctors. They tried to help me. All of my children came with me to the United States. They now have a good life. They go to school and have food to eat.

Name: Jeanine Nyakirindo

I was born in Uvira, Congo January 1st,1984. I was baptized in 1990. After I was baptized, I grew up in church, and joined a children's choir when I was 15 years old. I made the decision myself to be faithful and follow Jesus.

In 2004, it was Thursday night around 11pm, I was in bed in my shelter. I was with my children in same bed. I heard shooting already, and the same time they shot my little son. We were both shot and I did recognize what happened. I lost my consciousness, fainted. The people rescued me and took me to the hospital. I tried to recognize things after two months. I ask people where I was and where I am now. They told me "you are in the hospital now." My husband was out of the shelter at that time when he come in to sleep. I did not know that then when the militia shot me and I lost consciousness. My husband, "I did not see again." I was separated from my children for the whole two months spent in the hospital.

I am now with some of my children. The little one who was shot is still in Burundi. He is almost four, but the US government told me because still in the hospital, afterward, when feeling better, they will bring my child here.

All my family is not here and some are still in a refuge camp in Burundi. My Mom and Dad are both refugees in Rowanda. I am not working now. Part of my intestines was removed and I now have a colostomy bag. I live in South Dakota. The problems I have are not healed. I need a doctor to care for my needs.

Name: Jerome Mutuirutsa

I was born in Uvira, Congo in January 1, 1955. I was baptized in 1967. Before I was baptized, I was Catholic and living in my own village. It was hard to find a Catholic women. I decide to become Christian and at that time I find a fiance.

After being Christian, I went to John's youth groups. That time we had a different preacher from another area. That was the time I became Christian myself.

The first war I saw "civil war" in 1964 to 1965. Many people in my tribe were killed. Some of them were pastors and evangelists.

In 2004, in Burundi, I was outside the refuge camp on a Thursday. When I came back to the shelter I was really tired. I did not talk too much and I went to bed at 10pm. My wife told me "heard shooting inside." I said no and maybe it was outside. My wife said, "no, heard many shots." I tried to open the door of the shelter. I saw many shelters burned by fire. I yelled out, "please leave we are under attack!" In our shelter, there was eight families. Nine people were killed in our shelter and many of them were wounded by fire.

Two of my daughters are still in Africa in refuge camp in Rowanda and Burundi. The grave site of the people who were killed that night are in Gatumba. The same area of the massacre. We are still raising funds for a memorial to be built.

I don't have a job because I am not able to speak English. I am old and it is hard to learn another language.

Thirty-five years ago our tribe was very powerful in prayer. I remember one day we were in a prayer room and God sent a message to us. Even today your tribe is up against the government and other ethnic tribes. The message from God was:

"Don't worry about what happened. One day, your children and grandchildren they are going to go together to same school with white people and the white people will be your neighbors."

The dream came true.

Name: Pastor Dieu-donne Mudage, Mugaju

Banyamulenge is one of the tribes in Democratic Republic of Congo, this community live in east province Bukavu. Historically Banyamulenge have been in Congo more than four hundred years ago. Banyamulenge people are pastoralist, who keep cattle, and farms, they live in mountains of Uvira. Banyamulenge is one of minority in the community among four hundred and fifty communities. Normally Banyamulenge like moving place to place because of green pastures for their cattle and fertile place for the crops, they like to stay in the village because of their cattle. Banyamulenge did not inter-marry with other tribes because of their traditional belief. Languages, spoken in Kinyamulenge as the local language, and Swahili as one of the national languages. The Congo has four national languages; Swahili in East, Kikongo in West, North Lingala, South Kiluba and one international language.

Munyamulenge has been victimized in the war and conflict which occurred since 1996 and 1998. The main reason for other community to accuse them is they normally said that Banyamulenge are not Congolese. They are foreigners from Rowanda and Burundi, because of our physiognomy or physical appearance. Banyamulenge are one of the Tutsi tribes in the Great Lakes Region, somehow Kinyamulenge sounds like Kirundi, Kinyarwanda from our neighboring countries Burundi and Rowanda. The problem has been there since Bubutiste Regime, ANZURUNIBEMBE, who was the speaker of the parliament. Bembe fought for this issue many years to see if the government can prove a Munyamulenge to be considered as a foreigner not as a citizen.

Many people from all over the world have heard news from the radio, television, newspaper, and internet, about what is happening in the Congo since 1996. The Congo has been fighting for the bad Governance and politics which roamed since then. Banyamulenge are being victimized by the calamity in the Congo, but in another land. Banyamulenge are people who are suffering more than the other communities in the Congo. They have been tortured, violated, abused, raped, and discriminated by their neighboring communities.

In the second war in 1998, in one day in the area called Bubembe; tree villages of Kabela, Bibokoboko and Bivumu, were attacked by Government Militia Troops. Bibokobogo had more than 250 people killed and others were taken into captivity in Tanzania. The people who escaped death tried to risk their life to flee to Minembwe and Mungoma. This was not easy for them to go all the way to Minembwe or Mungoma. The reason is that on the way to both Monembwe and Mungoma the militia were scattered all over the area. The people had to find another way to escape the rebels. Women, children, older people and their cattle were killed. During that time it was the rainy season. Imagine all of this happening in that time. In the Dobo forest, many people lost their loved ones especially pregnant women, their children and older relatives. In the rain, no food, fire, or blankets to cover with for seven days in the forest. Normally the trip took two days on foot but this trip lasted more than a week.

The group of Banyamulenge refugees who are living in Nairobi, Kenya were among the group who escaped the tragedy in Bibokoboko. They received information about their friends who were taken by Wabembe to Tanzania. Some who were still alive tried to see which way they came back. Some of the group were saved; one lady and her two children along with four young people. No others were found. This is the reason why some of the Banyamulenge community still were negotiating with the Babembe community who were possibly holding some of the group as prisoners.

May God have mercy and grace for the people who are always negative to other human life. All were created by God in his own likeness. (Genesis 1:27) "So God created man in his own image; in his image he created male and female."(NIV)

I can say that some people have lost humanity in their heart. They are full of evil, envy, and hatred, which has packed their mind and heart. No more mercy and pity to the human being in today's life. In human nature we do have a superiority complex toward other human beings which I can call it wrong. All of us are equal and no one is special over the other. We have the same flesh, body, and blood. We are born in the same way where not one person should boast over the other. Nobody chooses to be who he or she is in person, tribe, race or color in this world. Everyone finds themselves and knows where they belong.

We as Christians believe that all people from race, color, and tribe are created by God without distinction. Second, we believe that God holds our destiny as our future. God loves us equally. God does not belong to any race or color in this world. Thirdly, Jesus, when he came to this world to save people, he did not come to some people by distinction of difference, race or color on this earth. Based on this reason we are required or re-commanded by God to love one another. (Matthew 22:36-39) "Sadducees and pharisees asked Jesus, 36. Teacher which is the great commandment in the Law? 37. Jesus replies: Love the Lord your God with all your heart and with all your soul and with all your mind. 38. This is the first and greatest commandment. 39. And the second is like it; love your neighbor as yourself." (NIV)

The situation in Eastern DR Congo are still very critical and sensitive to the people. The population does not have any idea on a solution on the conflict which has been there for a decade and three years. The situation, instead of changing for the better, is becoming worse and more complicated in the country. People have lost trust and hope to the politicians that are currently in office. The Banyamulenge people have many questions in their mind now for life, and how their land will be for the future.

My suggestion to the Congolese Government is to stop the war. Using people to kill one another is against humanitarian interest. Bad politics will not help, because many innocent lives are lost for no reason. Many women, children, and older people are victimized. Kindly, as the Government take responsibility to initiate a structure which this will bring peace to the people. Also, teach unity, and harmony among the Congolese, so that people can live and stay together as brothers and sisters in their beautiful country, the Congo.

My wishes is to see people from all over the world to help the Banyamulenge have peace with the neighboring communities and feel included in the Congolese society. May God help and bless the people who will be involved to see peace for the conflict resolution of the Banyamulenge community.

Pastor Mudage-Dieu-donne, Mugaju has a Bachelor of Arts in Religious Education from the East Africa School of Theology in Nairobi, Kenya.

Name: Prudence Munyakuri Nzigiye

I was born December 25, 1960 in the city of Minembwe, the territory of Fizi, and the country of the Congo DRC.

In the reign of Mobutu, our youth had to make an obligation commitment to be in the army, but the people did not want to go into the army. In 1996, in October President Mobutu made rules for the extermination of everyone who spoke Kinyarwanda language. He made a rule that in thirty one days 11/31/1996 every Congolese must come together to be killed. The law emphasized that all Tutsi, especially those who speak Kinyarwanda. By November 31, 1996, there should not be no Tutsi on Congolese land. The people who survive the killing should go back to Rowanda. Historically, this was originated from the fact that Belgian colonials while establishing country borders, they transferred a big part of what was Rowanda at the time to the Congo. This unfair border placement was due to the fact that Belgians needed this region because it was rich with minerals. The Bantus population were very strong and they could work in the mines. The plan had benefits for the Belgians but at the same time the Tutsi people were victims. This was not God's plan because God never created people without a home. One can question which development the Belgians brought to the Congo.

My mother died giving birth to my younger brother who was two years younger than me. We lived together with other Congolese who spoke many other languages. In the Congo, there are four hundred and fifty languages as well as tribes. In my tribe, we spoke the kinyarwanda language.

Since the Congo's independence, the tribe who spoke kinyarwanda became a problem. Every president who took power since then stated that our tribe are strangers. From 1960, Lumumba's presidency, Laurent Desire Kabila became a rebel to the government. However, his rebellion was a threat to my tribe because he wanted to take over all we owned. In addition, he wanted our men in our tribe to help by joining his rebellion. At this time my tribe took refuge in Uvira. Since then, we never stayed peacefully, we were refugees here and there. Being Christians, my parents and family were blessed and God provided food and home to us. This strengthened my belief and every time I remember the gospel message which says, "Who can be against us if God is for us?"

In the Refugee camp in Burundi, in Gatumba, Bujumbura. Many people were killed by rebels and I lost my last born daughter in this massacre. People were burnt, and exhausted, but the hand of God protected me in the intensive gun fire shots.

I have seen the hand of God protecting and guiding my family to Rwanda. Now, Rwanda is a peaceful African nation. Rwanda was a blessed nation which received peace from God.

After the Genocide in Gatumba, I moved to Rwanda. The Methodist Church chose a leader. The leaders select eight people and one is chosen. I was chosen. God had plans for me. Any time I pray, God knows and understands our situation in life.

My life in the Congo (DRC)

I am the first child of my father. My father had four sisters and no brothers. One of his sisters was married.

In 1967 to 1971, I went to school by foot six kilometers. We did not have a car and the school was Runundu Center. We lived in Monyi, Minembwe.

In 1974, I lived in Rugaraba, and finished my primary school at Kamombo. The secondary school I attended was a 120 kilometer walk on foot. It became too far and I changed schools to Mboko which is a 60 kilometer walk from 1975 to 1978. In 1978 to 1990, I went to Bible school in Mushimbakye, Baraka. In 1990, I started teaching primary school which is five grade levels at Methodist Mitamba and Mukumba. I taught for free, the government does not pay salary to teachers. In July 1990 to 2004, I started a business to sell cows. My farm had fifty cows.

In the night of August 13th and 14th 2004, at the Burundi and Gatumba refuge camps, the rebels from the Congo Government, Army, FDLR and FNL coalition killed one hundred and sixty five people. My daughter and niece were killed there. One hundred and ten were wounded and had to be treated at the hospital. We left Burundi in Rwanda, Kigali. I was working in Church Free Methodist/Kiyovu from January 1, 2005 to December 30, 2006. We came back to Burundi for interview to come to the United States of America April 3rd and 4th 2007. This is a miracle of God, I did not think or plan to live in America. My pockets were empty, no money to buy passport or visa, no money to fly from Africa to the United States. I never dreamed that I could become a resident of the United States of America.

Every time I pray to God, he knows everyone and understands our prayer. I made a budget in 2007 for my family. We had enough money to pay rent, to put money aside for scholarship for my children, buy clothes for my family, to provide food for everyone and to have a bank account. I am sorrowful, yet always rejoicing, poor, yet making possessing everything. After planning the budget, I called my spouse and my children, to come pray for this budget. God is the answer to our prayers. 2 Corinthians 6:3-10. The same day God made plans for everything in our prayer. My dream doesn't plan for leaving Rwanda to America where I am today with my family. In August 22, 2007, I was in an accident and almost died. I was in the hospital for a month and three weeks. God gave me my life back. He watches over us and is our provider for all our needs.

Name: Dollard Mazimano

My name is Dollard Mazimano, I was born in 1989 in the Democratic Republic of Congo. I'm currently living in Missouri and I'm a sophomore at Central Methodist University, majoring in Human Service. I have both parents and six siblings, but two passed away during the war in 1998. The Congo contains more than 340 tribes, but the tribe which I come from is called the Banyamulenge. I have been separated from my family for five years, from 1998 to 2003. The Banyamulenge, Tutsi are pastoralists living in the high plateau region of south Kivu, in eastern Congo. Since the war started in 1997, the civilians in the Congo remain victims of mass killings and torture. After the peace agreement was made in 2003 between the various rebel movements and the Congolese government. The Congolese Tutsis hoped that they would no longer be discriminated against and subject to violence. By 2004, these hopes had evaporated as elements in the government conspired with extremist politicians from the eastern part of the Congo to increase hostility towards the Tutsis in the east. 250,000 thousand people have been displaced in 2008 alone and many others had died in violence between government forces and rebel militants in the region of South Kivu. During the night of August 13, 2004, about 166 people from my tribe were mercilessly slaughtered and 116 were left wounded by the armed factions in the refugee camp called "Gatumba." Many Banyamulenge citizens and refugees who now live in different parts of Africa, continues to live in danger and have no one to speak on their behalf. Lubumbashi, Likasi and many other Congolese cities were the first to be attacked in 1998. Many people were killed or imprisoned, in some cases (prisoners for their own safety). My family was among other families who were held as prisoners in Lubumbashi. It was not safe or healthy to live in the prison, we did not know whether we were going to be killed or released. We ate once a day, slept on the floor and had no medical help until we were recognized by the non profit organizations. A year later, we were released, but my mother and older brother were taken into a different country than me and the rest of my siblings. My father was in a different Provence than the rest of my family when the war started, for a long time we did not know it he was alive or dead. It was very difficult living without a mother or father. My sister who was fifteen years old at the time, took care of me and my younger brother until my older sister who was to marry, came to join us two years later. For a long four years I did not see my mother until we were united in 2003, in the United States. I was just a young innocent girl when we were kicked out of the Congo, I didn't understand why we had been locked away or why my mother had to stay behind. I would like to see the United Nations take a stand to stop the war that is going on in my country. Food, medications, and security continue to be their main concern for the killing in South Kivu continues as we speak today. Parents have no jobs, children are unable to receive education, and people are dying from hunger and diseases. Many African government systems are epileptic, rigid, and rival with others which leads to the loss of many innocent lives. From 2001 to the present, the United States accepted for resettlement of some of the prisoners and refugee families, who had been referred to the United States. Many children today are going through the same thing and have no hope of a better future. Refugees and survivors are unable to return to their homes because of the ongoing violence against them in the Congo and have fear for their lives because some countries are demanding them to return to their own country.

The second best solution is for the refugees to integrate into the communities where they have fled. These are often places that are familiar to them in terms of landscape, language, and lifestyle.

The third solution is for the refugees to resettle in a third country. While some survivors were settled by UNHCR in other refugee camps in Burundi, including Mwaro and Gasorwe. Other refugees were understandably fearful of going to another refugee camp and chose instead to provide for themselves in Bujumbura. Some families split up with different members going to different places.

Name: Jolie Uzamukunda

My name is Jolie Uzamukunda and I am a junior at Eastern Nazarene College. I was born and raised in the Democratic Republic of Congo. I belong to an ethnic group called Banyamulenge which can simply describe as Tutsi Rwandans who moved to South Kivu in the eastern region of the Congo about five centuries ago. This has both negative and positive impact in my life.

The negative side was the problem I had to face as a Munyamulenge. The only home that I knew was is South Kivu of the Congo, but this is why the government and some ethnic groups never accept us as part of the Congolese citizens which was a question I always have in my mind. The government of the Congo wanted Banyamulenge to return to their country because they believed that we had no rights to live in the Congo as other Congolese. Because of this issue, many of the Banyamulenge were killed in different wars.

The recent war was in Burundi where they killed about 300 people who were in the refugee camp.

In a positive side, most of the Banyamulenge people are Christians and they always start churches no matter where they go. They have many churches in Rwanda, Burundi, Uganda, Kenya, Europe and the United States. We live by the verse in the Bible (Mark 16:15) that says "As you go into the entire world, proclaim the gospel to everyone." This is what Jesus told his disciples and it is the reason why many Banyamulenge never stop preaching the gospel wherever they go. As a Munyamulenge, my goal to let the whole world know who my Jesus is and what he has done in my life. In conclusion, my dream is that one day I would see Banyamulenge people have their own country, a place they call home, and where they have freedom like other citizens.

Name: Alexis R. Mbagariye

I am a native of the Democratic Republic of the Congo, in the eastern district of South Kivu, precisely in the high mountains of Mulenge, Rurambo Village. At this time I am a permanent resident of the United States and I have received my undergraduate degree from the University of Maryland College Park. I am pursuing my master degree in Public Administration and project Management.

From the time I was growing up to the late seventies, there has been animosity between my community Banyamulenge Tutsi tribe and the rest of the other tribes we lived with notably the Bafuliru, Banyindu, Bashi, and Babembe. The hostilities primarily political reasons fueled by local and central government.

I remember in the Summer of 1993 when I was in Kalemie town, in the Katanga district passing my high school national exam. I was detained in a police cell for 24 hours simply because I walked in a place where other people were walking. The police who arrested me said that I was not supposed to walk in that particular area. When I asked why, they placed me in jail. My friends were notified and they paid money for my release from jail.

The Banyamulenge Tutsi tribe lived in the DRC for over two centuries. Some of the tribe held high positions in the government such as Vice President of the Republic of Congo as well as potential candidates for Presidential elections. Other positions held were Generals in the army, Senators, and Vice Governors. We have been accused of being citizens of Rwanda and this led to many crimes against humanity which has caused a "genocide" among the Banyamulenge Tutsi tribe.

The end result has caused many Banyamulenge people to be scattered all over the world. Some in the neighboring countries such as Burundi where in August 2004 they were attacked and killed selectively in the Gatumba refugee camp.

The DRC government must treat it's citizens equally. We need PEACE now!

Name: Emmanuel Nkundimana, Mihingana

I am Emmanuel Nkundimana, Mihingana and I was born in the Democratic Republic of the Congo on January 1st 1951. I was baptized on May 6th 1966. After getting saved I was baptized in the spirit then I was called to serve the Lord. My call started as an evangelist in 1970 to 1978. In 1979 I was appointed as a local church leader and in 1983, I was promoted to be the chairman of the Anglican churches in Shaba subregion till 1998 when the Democratic Republic of Congo went to war.

I would like to give you a summary of mistreatments of the Banyamulenge tribe in the Congo Kinshasa. The war started in 1964 when I was a boy and I was in my 3rd year of schooling. The rebels started a movement that turned into a movement in fighting the Banyamulenge tribe among the other Congolese. The tribe I belong is still being mistreated in that country. Ngatongo in Fizi County was the first village to be attacked and many people lost their lives. They were cut by machete and other harmful tools with hands tied in the back. The Kirumba village men and women were massacred only for their physical appearance. Among those killed were Rupembwe, Nyabuhuga, and Muganwapastors who were fighting against discrimination and mistreatments. Some tribe leaders were killed too during this event and they are Mushishi, Karaha, and other wise people. They are Bitebetebe, Budutira, Rutegeranya and Ruregeya.

The selective discrimination continued up to Mobutu leadership. Our tribe could not own anything at all. We were sent to jail and our property was taken from us. We are foreigners in our own country. We were not considered as citizens by the government. We did not have anyone to protect us.

The genocide continued in Bubembe villages in 1996. The villages are Magunga and Bibogobogo. The people captured were taken to enemy villages named Baraka where they were mistreated, others were killed, and some were taken as slaves. Women were raped in front of their families. Others were stoned or shot down by powerful guns.

In 1998, we were living in Shaba, Katanga province. The massacre started in Tanganyika sub province known as Kalemie. They entered the village by night and selected Banyamulenge people in the city. Men, women and children were killed and some sent to jail.

I was the pastor who signed letters that would accompany the dead bodies to South Kivu province. Their bodies were respectfully buried in Uvira.

The worst event extended to Kamina Oromani in Katanga province, where all soldiers from Banyamulenge tribe were killed. Some escaped and were in the Burundi refugee camp.

The massive killing continued in Lubumbashi, Likasi, and Kamina. They were killed by burnt tires and there were many witnesses who experienced that event. Some of the survivors who were witnesses now live in the United States and other refugee camps in Africa.

In August 1998, the war reached our village Myura in the Moba county intersection of Kalemie County and Moba County. The war started when the foreign minister spoke to the media on killing the Banyamulenge people in the entire country. In August 15th 1998 men, women, and children were locked in churches and schools waiting to be executed. Some people escaped and hid in the forest scared and hopeless in being killed by the government.

We prayed to God for all of this killing to stop. I was not in the refugee camp in Gatumba when the tragic massacre on August 13th 2004 killed 165 and seriously injured 120 others.

God gave me nine children: four boys and five girls. I came with six children: three boys and three girls. Three of my children are still in Africa and are married: one boy and two girls. We pray to God that one day we will be reunited as a family. We believe in God that will happen.

I strongly feel that we need to rescue the orphans who are still alive. I want to feel that there is hope and security because I am in a peaceful country. Whenever I remember the widows and orphans my happiness changes to sadness and I cannot sleep thinking about those survivors. I asked myself what I can do to help those in danger and I came up with the idea; help, rescue, and protect. In help: we seek those surviving orphans and widows. In rescue: to search for survivors whose lives are in danger. In protection: we have to stand firm and fight against any discrimination by reconciliation as a way to reach peace.

I was so excited to see that there are some people who have the positive attitude toward those survivors and lets me believe that we can save others in danger. When we gather our ideas and efforts, we can make a life changing difference in one life at a time.

Finally, we greet you in the Lord's name and wish you success of our dreams.

Name: David Byiringiro

My name is David Byirngiro. I was born and raised in January 1st 1987 in the Uvira village. I am from the Banyamulenge tribe. I am the twelfth child in my family. In 1995, I left my country to be refugee in Rwanda, because our tribe was in torture by the Congo government. I was separated from my parents that time. They stayed in the Congo because of the hard times they had. My Mom and two of my brothers died.

After a few years being a refugee in Rwanda, I decided to go back to Burundi Refugee camp. We had a massacre in 2004, one of my nieces was killed. My sister was shot in her right hand and is paralyzed, along with other problems. My request is to ask the United Nations to help our tribe have peace and be treated like human beings. We also want to be recognized as citizens in the Congo.

Name: Pappy Amani

First of all my name is Pappy Amani and I'm from Democratic Republic of the Congo in Uvira. Since I was born, I have never been to another country in Africa, or the United States. My first time I went in Burundi in 2005 is because of the wars in the Congo. After two months Burundi's UNHCR decided to take me to the refugee camp in Mwaro. I have been in the camp almost two years and was going to be resettled in the United States of America. I passed all the interviews and was ready to go. Right now I live in the United States. There are a lot of problems in the DR Congo, but I am going to discuss four that stand out the most. The problems are wars, political disorganization, too many tribes, and education.

In my opinion there are serious problems that affect the country and the Congolese people. People still move up to other countries because of the war that is in the eastern part of DR Congo. Please we need help so we can live our life in peace in our own land.

Name: Antoine Ndasumbwa

I was born in 1950 in the Congo. I was baptized in 1968 and this is the time I was changed and born again. I received Jesus Christ as my savior. My life after genocide in 2004 in Bujumbura or Gatumba Refugee camp. It was terrible, I have never seen this before in my life. In the 13th of August 2004 in the middle of the night, I was shot in my head and I lost consciousness. I went into a coma for three weeks. The people tried to take me to Bujumbara Hospital, but the Doctor was not able to do what was needed and they decided to transfer me to Kenya General Hospital. I spent almost one week and my consciousness came back. My right hand and leg was paralyzed. This happened because I was wounded in a bad spot in my head. I spent three months in Kenya and I come back to Burundi and HCR took me to their refugee camp. I could not stay there because of my injury and they decided to take me out of the camp. Now I am in Bujumbura town, but I am still sick. Once the people went thru the inter-view to take them to the United States. I was unconscious at the time. My kids are still close which means I need the HCR to accept me to go to the United States to be treated. I have my Doctor report and I wrote them a letter about my condi-tion. I have not received an answer yet. I have seven children and two orphans because of my one daughter who was killed the same night I was shot. She left me two children. All of my family is in refugee camp in Bujumbura. I am struggling right now and I cannot sleep. I am living a hard life now. We need help.

Name: Miriam Nyamusaraba

I was born in the Congo in 1959. I was baptized, but can't remember the date. I do know I was changed when I received Jesus Christ.

My life after August 13th 2004 in the refugee camp is very hard to explain, because I lost my family. My daughter was killed in the same camp and my husband is one who is paralyzed . I can't do anything because I care for my husband. The two orphan children left by my daughter are still young which means I care for them at home. I have no money to take the children to preschool.

In our shelter, I see many people who were wounded. They were shot and it is a big problem in my heart. Once I remember of all of the shooting and killing, I am not able to sleep or do anything. Now, we are in a hard situation. We need HCR to open our case and go to be treated in the United States. Any help, please God! God Bless You.

Name: Alexis Shandata

I was born in 1974 in the Congo in Rurambo Village. I have five children, three boys and two girls. I was baptized and did receive Jesus Christ as my Savior. I came to be a refugee in Burundi in 2000 and I was outside the refugee camp. This was the night people were killed. God protected my family, no one was killed in my family. After the genocide, I had something like fear in my life. It took me a week to overcome. In 2006, one of my legs was cold, but one day my leg from knee down was moving involuntarily and they took me to a hospital. The doctor said this has never happened and they decided to cut the leg off in 2006.

Right now, I have pain and my life as a refugee is difficult. I cannot do anything till I am treated. If someone can have compassion to help me get treated to have a leg prosthesis or a wheelchair. Also, to help my children because they are living a hard life. God Bless Them! God Bless You!

Name: Francoise Bikundwa

I was born in the Congo in 1975. I have four children. I was baptized and received Jesus Christ. I am a Christian now.

My life after Genocide in the Congo, as I remember the things that happened to me. Sometimes I lose my mind, I was just married two years and the war had started in the Congo. The Congo government decided to kill us. I remember the speech given by some of the political men from the Congo. They said, "Kill, Kill every Bunyamolenge!" The militia come in our house and they took everything in our house. They took us to jail. Many people were killed by shooting and by knife. So many girls were raped until they died. One girl was raped by ten men. They took me to Bakita prison for thirteen months. My first born was born in jail. That time I did not have access to water, medicine, or food. I can say for every woman being pregnant how we felt. We felt hungry, the need to use toilet, and the struggle with sickness. All things said, I was in jail, in a small room without sleep and not able to move. "I cannot get out." It was a big problem in my life.

I delivered myself, my daughter by myself. No nurse, no doctor, or anybody. I cut the cord with my teeth. God protected myself and my children right now. I am struggling right now in refugee camp in Kenya. I need all kinds of help, any kind of help for my children. Many people with me were in jail the same time. They need help also to come to United States. Thank you for your help.

Name: Alexis Mugabo

I was born in 1983 in the Congo. I was baptized in 1991 and felt changed in 2006. In 2006, I decided to accept Jesus Christ as my Savior. I have seen so many things happen to my tribe. I saw people wounded, killed, and villages destroyed by young militia.

The war in 1998, the people left their home in the Congo. I saw people die of hunger and heavy rains killing men, women and children. The people did not have shelter for cover from the heavy rains and cold air.

In 2004, I decided to leave the country and go into the refugee camp in Rwanda. I spent two years there and decided to go to another refugee camp in Kampala, in Uganda. I am looking if I can have peace and continue my studies, because my country denied our citizenship. I have two children and four orphans.

Now, I am not with all of my family. Some are staying in Bujumbura refugee camp and others are in the refugee camp in Rwanda. I am in a serious situation for help. You can use my name in your book.

Name: Chantal Nyiramazaire

I was born in 1975 in the Congo and baptized in 1996. In my heart, I was changed and born again in 2002. I heard a voice inside me and it said, "you are saved."

When I was born, all my family was catholic. I stayed there in same church and one time voice come to me to be baptized. I come to Rwanda in 1998. When the Congo was in trouble, my heart was open to do something, but I did not get a chance to go to school. I asked God what I can do without an education, or whom can understand me? God said, "Even you do not have an education, I am with you." That time, I started a little group for prayer. I told people to pray for the situation happening in the Congo, and in Rwanda too. Rwanda was struggling after genocide and many people had a broken heart. I moved to Rwamagana and we started a small local church. I told the Pastor that God told me that you can start the church and I could support the church by prayer. The church's name is Restoration Church to restoration of the people with a broken heart. I stayed there almost six years and I have been sick for a long time. When I went to the hospital the Doctor said he did not find anything. I decide to pray by myself and the voice came again to me. The voice said, "you remember I put the Congo in your heart, now you have to move to pray for the country even though the situation is still bad, but I promise you I will protect you." Then, I went there, after I arrive in Minembwe. I start to preach to people forgiveness and to pray that the Congo can have peace. God put the burden on my heart.

I am not married, but I give my life to the Congo. I want to pray to seek peace and reconciliation to the people. It is hard for me to leave and things happen, but God needs me to do something for country. I have this calling and this dream.

The problem is I have challenges for the people who do not have an education, they are poor, and have disease. They are hungry, and do not have a place to worship God. We worship outside. There is no toilet and no water in the village. The people still go to the river. These type of needs are problems and the people do not understand what God wants from the Congo. We need all kinds of help for the people and the Congo.

Name: Pastor Pierre Nzamu

I was born in 1914, and baptized in 1950. In 1947, I heard a voice call and he said, "I want to use you to be the light to save your tribe." This was new to me and I did not accept quickly. I waited until 1950, the time I decided to be baptized. It was very hard because all our tribe was denied for anyone to eat meat, chicken and goat. In 1914 to 1950, we were unable to eat meat, unable to have religion, and everything which was taboo. People who came from Europe brought religion and was able to break taboo. If you accepted to break taboo you were denied from the tribe. It was hard to make a decision.

In 1953, I became the preacher and that was time I tried to preach my tribe. Many people accepted Jesus Christ and they were baptized. I was one of few people who brought salvation to our tribe.

In 1960, many people decided not to follow Jesus Christ. I preached to them to come back for salvation and Jesus Christ helped me. I do the best I can for my tribe and they were saved again. That is why when I am now old that God protect me to see the fruit of my work. The many fruit I see with the people who want to become pastor. God is showing me the fruit of my work. Even right now all the times I preach to my tribe, it is a success for me. He said, " it's my award." Matthew 3:1&2 states, "In those days John the Baptist came preaching in the wilderness of Judea,2"Repent for the kingdom of heaven is at hand." Once I die my people will have read Matthew 3:1-5 which states, "In those days John the Baptist came preaching in the wilderness of Judea, 2"Repent for the kingdom of heaven is at hand." 3For this is he who has spoken of by the prophet Isaiah when he said, "The voice of one crying in the wilderness: "prepare the way of the Lord; make his paths straight." 4Now John wore a garment of camel's hair and a leather belt around his waist, and his food was locusts and wild honey. 5 Then Jerusalem and all Judea and all the region about the Jordan were going out to him," All my people are going to read that book, "my legacy."

We struggle with school, during that time, in the sixties, because there was no chalk board or board to explain the lessons. All lessons were written on clothes which meant it was very hard to accept in being a student.

We met many wars in the Congo. I saw many many people die. Many children, women, men, and pastors die, but we never give up preaching and praying for the Congo. Even now, at age 95 years old, I am still praying for my country and my tribe. I am praying we have peace and to pray for the country in general. He said, "God bless my generation who work hard for our tribe to be saved and this generation now who accept and support us in our old age."

I can't imagine how young man Laurent came from United States to see me. I did not know him only because I worked with his parents. God bless you and God bless your calling.

Name: Pastor Adrien Kajabika

I was born in 1925 in Fizi, a village in the Congo. I was baptized in 1945, in Remera Cepac. I left Lubuga after the baptism.

When I was a teenager, I went to the farm with other people the same age and other parents. I was in one village called Kajembwe, in dream I fell down after I felt fear. The day after I told other people we were together on farm. I had a dream, but sounds to me a fear I can do nothing. Another night I had the same dream but, it was different. First, I heard a voice say, "you die." When I woke up, I am still alive. I told the people the fear come in my heart. This fear stayed with me for one year while I worked on the farm. I asked my friend why did the Pigme Tribe leave? They live in the forest. They wear leaves for clothes. I could go there to see the tribal doctor to tell what fear I have. He told me the place and I went there. They, the Slave tribe, received me. I told him the dream and about my fear I had, but he did not give me an answer or any traditional medication. Then, I decided to come back home. One evening, I met some young boy, he held something in his hand. I asked, "what are you holding?" It was the year 1942. He told me, "this is a book you can read and you can know about God and Jesus. Then after that, you can have eternal life. You cannot die, if you trust the scriptures." I ask, what you say, now, myself I cannot die anymore, this is the medicine I needed. The same evening, I received joy in my heart. For many years, I was lost, no hope, only fear was in my life and heart. For me, the same day, I received Jesus in my heart. My salvation. From that time, I feel thirsty in my heart to want additional information from the book. I found one man from Rwanda and he told me this is the Bible. I asked him the question on how I read the Bible, because this book is the word of God. I cannot read. I don't know how. He told me that he will try to teach me to read and write. That time I started the ABC's until God helped me. I started to know how to read the Bible. We decide to go to baptize with another man called "Matayo." We went to Remera to be baptized. We found an Evangelist and he asked a question. He said, "Are you able to read and write? We cannot baptize anyone who cannot read the Bible." We said, "yes." We was aware, before baptism, we wore jewelry on our neck and wrist from our tribe. Once baptized, we do not wear any jewelry from tradition. He said to me, Matayo, and one woman, named Elizabeth Kibihira, we are the first in our tribe to be baptized and receive Jesus Christ. The same evening, after baptism, I received two baptisms. Once immersed in the river, to go down and raise up, he started speaking in tongues which all day and night.

From that day, Jesus called us the three to bring good news of Jesus Christ in our Banyamulenge tribe. We had a difficult time, because we were supposed to put God in our tribe and tear down the tribal belief of the worship of many gods to only have one God.

We invite many people to come into the tribe, a new crusade. This same day, many people received Christ as our Lord and Savior. The first time for our tribe to accept the calling of God and to recognize the Gospel, the Bible and repentance. Many of our children, young boys and girls accepted Christ and were baptized.

Now, I am still living, I am 84, and God promised us not die, but to tell the people the goodness of our God. I am very proud to receive Laurent in my house. We share this faith and all things all things he ask me about the book. I wish everybody can read this book and understand our calling. It was very hard but, now we see the fruits for all we preached in our tribe. For me, this is a sign from Jesus. We did note dreams about book and about our tribe. If we can have someone who can write down about all things we went through, because our education was dark, we did not go to school. God is good and he told me even we can die today. "Me (myself), your Dad, and my Dad, we think is very nice. We can die in peace, because we left something for us to read."

Name: Olivier Munezero

My name is Oliver Munezero and I was born in the Congo in 1985. The village I was born is Vyura. I was baptized in 1995. In 1998, we were in that village living peacefully. One night we saw the militia surrounding all the mountain area and they blocked the road. "No one can go out of village or come in because this is your day to be killed. This is your Apocalypse Day," quoted, the announcement.

The day they took all the people together. They separated the men from age 20 to 80. They put them in a big church. Then, they took young and older women and children and put them in a big school area. They said, "you will be killed the same day." They tried to take some of the men and women to be killed outside and others tortured. The women were raped and tortured the same day. After one week, God sent a miracle and we saw the army from Rwanda come this same day and they attacked the militia surrounding the church and school. The militia left and we were delivered. That day they decided to take us out of the city. It was hard because we were supposed to walk seven days to Kalemi Town. After being in Kalemi Town, we were to take a boat to go to Uvira. Many older people and children died because of the long walk.

Now, I still have a problem with all my family still in Mwaro Refugee camp. They are struggling with big issues of Burundi government. They spend one week without food, water, or medicine.

I request that the United Nations and the United States take this issue seriously and the people have compassion to help orphans and widows of my tribe. Thank you for Laurent and Debbie to let people know in this book.

Name: Angelique Nyankamirwa

I was born in 1960, in the Congo in the village of Gahuna. I was baptized in 1972 in the Congo. The church name was Bijombo. It was very hard to be baptized, because both my parents was catholic. They do not believe in the immersion baptism. We decided with other children to find salvation ourself. We were baptized on our own without telling our parents. After baptism, my parents said we no longer live in our house. I decided to go live with my grandparents. That time our parents beat children and they suffered, but was strong in salvation.

Before 2004 in genocide, I lived in refugee camp for ten years. In 1994, my husband was killed by the Congo government without any reason, only because we looked like Tutsi. They said my husband died young only after few years married with two children. A boy and girl. Raising children as a widow without any income is very hard, no money. After that, I took my youngest son and give him arrangement at age of seventeen. That son would take the place of Dad that was killed. Now, in 2004, we left our country and we go to Burundi Refugee camp. One night at around 10pm August 13th, the militia come. The first thing they do in my shelter, they shot my own son and he died with his wife, children, grandchildren. They put fire on everybody. In our shelter, many people died that night. I remember Gatoni with two children died that night.

My family is not together, because my daughter is still in Burundi Refugee camp. The night of the massacre, I was separated from my daughter. Now, in January 18th, 2010, I know three weeks ago, I was notified that my daughter is alive in Burundi. She is having a hard time because she was traumatized from that horrible day. Please, I need help and I would like for my daughter to live with me in Colorado.

I have four children who are orphans. I came to Colorado with them. I am the mother, grandmother, and father, to these children. One of my orphans, is a girl who is badly burned and needs medical attention to make her well. She needs plastic surgery for the bad burns. The scaring of the burn is in back of her head and down her chest, and back of one leg. Please, if your project can bring the reunion of my family in Colorado.

Name: Mechec Sebatunzi

My name is Mechec Sebatunzi and I was born in December 25th 1952, in the Congo. I was baptized in Bigombo in 1963 during the time when racism was bad for our tribe. This is when there was a war in Bigombo.

In 1998, there was a big war in the Congo against our tribe. I remember in July 5th,1998, the Congo government gave an announcement Tuesday, Wednesday, and Thursday consecutively. They said, "kill every Tutsi." The same day I was coming from a house sale, farm market. They attacked us, many of the people, some were my friends died immediately because I had money. They said, "do not kill the man with money because he might have another source of money elsewhere." They take me captive with my money and put me in jail. I was placed in a jail with many people I knew. We spend mostly one month without clothes, water, and only gave a small amount of food each day. We had been tortured and I never experienced this before. They beat all of us in jail and many started to die.

We were placed in two different jails. We spent thirteen months in jail without seeing family. No freedom to go outside, no food, no water, and no medical attention. We had people die each day. I remember Samuel Sadoki, Rwiyereka, and Rutandara. They were all killed.

I spent almost six years without seeing my family. The United Nations took me from jail to go to Texas. I did not get a chance to go to school. It was hard for me to explain how my wife and children can join me in Texas, but God is good. One of my caseworkers tried to help me until my family did come to Texas in 2004.

The only problem I have is I left two children in Africa. I am looking in to how I can get my children home in Texas. Hopefully, this book will help us join our family.

Name: Iragaba Runezerwa

My name is Iragaba Runezerwa. My family has thirteen members, four boys, and seven girls. I was born in 1951, in the Congo. I was baptized in 1966, in Uvira. This is the time I was changed and became a real Christian.

I want to talk about the war in 2002. I lived in Uvira and this was the same time the Congo government said, "Kill every Munyamulenge, Kill every Munyamulenge in area!" Many of the people died that time. Other people were badly injured, involving a leg or arm injury. That was the time I decided to leave the Congo and go to Burundi refugee camp. I stayed there two years. Then, in August 13th,2004, it was night around 10pm, I was with my family during prayer. We heard the guns, the militia was singing, which was a way to confuse us. Many people were listening to the song thinking it was people singing and praying. It's in our culture to sing and pray every night. I was in shelter number eight. I heard two of my children and my wife was shot with a gun. Then, in our shelter four people died immediately. I remember one woman and her two boys died that same day. It was a terrible day, how people were killed in our refugee camp, because how they look, and how God created them.

I bring all my family here and I only left two orphans, from my brother, who was killed that same night. These two children are in refugee camp in Nayrobi, Kenya. I am not working now, because I am not able to learn English. I did not get a chance to go to school in Africa. If you would please help the orphans and widows in the refugee camp. Thank you and God bless you.

Name: Feza Nyamutigerwa

My name is Feza Nyamutigerwa. I was born in 1984, in the Congo. I have eight children. The reason why I need to give my testimonial is because I have sorrow in my heart for many years. I left my family when I was ten years old. Now, I am twenty four years old and I never saw my family any more. I live in South Dakota, without my family. I never see anybody I know.

In 1998, the war started, when I was with my mother's sister. The government said, "Kill every Munyimulenge." The militia came to our house and took us to jail. We spent one year in jail. Many people were killed, tortured, and others were badly burned by fire.

I am not educated because of war. This makes me feel bad, and not of any value. I wish all the children in the Congo and refugee camp to get educational assistance. If possible, please help me find my family. I would like my family to live where I am in South Dakota. I am like an orphan, but my parents are still alive. Please find them!

When I work, I remember my family and I cry. People ask me," why, what's wrong?" Maybe, people think it is hard for me to live without family. When I remember, I see there faces and I cry. Please! Please! I want to be united with my family. Maybe, the book will unite me with my family in the United States.

Name: Jolie Mirika

My name is Jolie Mirika and I was born in January 1st,1989, in the Congo. We have five children, including me in my family. I was in shelter number two in refugee camp in Burundi. It was 10pm, we were outside singing and giving praises. Many young boys and sisters sing together in a choir. When we finished our practice, one of our leaders prayed for us. She said, "go home, and we will meet Saturday." Just as I arrived at the shelter, I was ready to go to bed. Then, we heard the guns, and my Dad ran fast and took the two children in his hand. Our shelter was in the back. The same time, Dad came back and told us, "go outside, we are being attacked!" In one minute, my mom was shot and killed along with my brother. My brother did not die. People were being shot and killed and burned. I ran, I miss my mom, I love her so much. I will never see her again, because after being shot, she was burned. I could not recognize her because she was badly burned. Sometimes if I remember her, I feel traumatized.

Now, my dad lives in Texas and three orphans are left behind. God bless and let many people know about us in this book.

Name: Fanny Nabagigi

My name is Fanny Nabagigi and I was born In 1990, in the Congo. I now live in South Dakota. I have two parents. We were in the refugee camp in 2004, gut God protected us. We did not lose anyone in my family.

The only thing I have to wish is I left many children my age. They are orphaned now without any assistance. Please, if you can help get them here, they can have education. Thank you for this opportunity.

Now, I am a choir member in South Dakota. I am still in high school.

Name: Daniella Namukobwa

My name is Daniella Namukobwa. I was born in January 1993 in the Congo. I was baptized in Bujumbura which is the capital of Burundi.

Our family has nine children, four boys and five girls. I am very young. I can't give all my testimony but, I can say a few things. I saw after genocide in Burundi, many of my friends same age die the same night, that I still remember.

Some are orphaned by now, they lost a parent, mother or father.

Now, after the United Nations take us to South Dakota. I am able to have clothes, food, medical treatment, lotion, soap, and water. I wish that those children who are suffering in refugee camp can be taken here to have an education and right to be here in the United States.

Name: Isaac Gapingi

My name is Isaac Gapingi and I was born January 1962. I cannot remember the exact date I was baptized. All of my children, and my wife were killed in August 2004. I am alone, by myself and I was shot in my shoulder in 2004. My right hand does not work well and I am unable to work. I was also shot at the top of my head.

Can you imagine how a father like me who lost his family and wife, no sickness, or accident, but killed. If I remember, I get upset and don't eat. If I think about them I stop every-thing. Now, I live by government assistance because I am not able to work. I only need the United Nations to bring my brother and his family to come and be with me in Iowa.

I wish the Congo government to recognize our citizen-ship and ask forgiveness to all innocent people who have been killed. God Bless You

Name: Joseph Rwibutso

My name is Joseph Rwibutso and I am Eighteen years old. I have my Mom and Dad and myself live in South Dakota. I also have three brothers and two sisters in my family.

The massacre in 2004 in Burundi, it was very terrible to tell other people. I saw many people my age and others who were older than me was crying about life. They were injured and burned. They say help but, we were unable to do anything for them. I think other people need to know what happened to our tribe. Then, maybe the Congo government will be able to stop the massacre of innocent people. Please help the orphans and people who are suffering.

Name: Teti Furaha

My name is Teti Furaha and I was born in January 1, 1993. We have nine children in our family. After the genocide in 2004 in Burundi, our life was very very hard. I thank God, because all the time God cannot leave us alone. Now, we are able to go to school, to have something to eat, and have freedom or right to get anything we want.

Here, I was separated from my family in September 1998 to now. I never see them again. But, I know they are in Kenya refugee camp.

I wish I can be able to have my family here because I now live with my brother. I need my Mother, Father, and siblings here. If possible, you can try to ask people for compassion to help those children, orphans, widows, and other people who are injured.

Name: Mutesi Nabitanga

My name is Mutesi Nabitanga. I was born in March 1991 in the Congo. I was baptized in Missouri. In our family, we have seven children; three girls, four boys. I was separated from my Father when I was seven years old, because of the war in 1998. My Father was shot in the leg and then they cut the leg off. Until now, I have one leg.

From 1998, we did not know if our father was still alive. Because my Dad was too far from us, the day he was shot. We did not have someone to tell us the information of what happened.

The situation with my Dad involved a white lady, who had compassion, helped my Dad. He was taken to Red Cross and the Red Cross decided to take him to Missouri. So we did not know where he would be after four years in the year 2000. He was able to tell people in Missouri even my leg is gone but, I have family with seven children still living in the Congo. The agency in Missouri tried to help my Dad find his family. God is good to see that he is alive and with us. Even he did not have his leg but, God Bless the United States. Now, we have a nice house and all the children go to school. My Mother and Dad both have a job.

Many years we wanted hope for our future. Now, we see the future in our family. God Bless the United Nations and the United States.

Name: Emmanuel Nkumdamahoro Mihingano

My name is Emmanuel Nkumdamahoro Mihingano and I was baptized June 6, 1965 in the Congo, in the village named Nganji. In that time I was being transformed, and baptized by the Holy Spirit.

Our tribe had a time when we were against other tribes in the Congo. The reason was because we were Tutsi, and second reason is because our tribe is responsible for the cows as farmers. The other tribes did not have the privilege of getting cows from us. The other tribes named Babembei, and Bashi attacked our tribe because of the cows. We had many many massacres, small groups of a hundred to as many as little to twenty killed at a time. In 1965, there was two villages, one called Kugatongo and Kirumba where many people and cows were killed. Some of the children were held captive at the time.

In 1996, a genocide of the two villages named Bubembe and Bibogobogo, five hundred were killed in that time. Many children were held captive until now 2010. We know children were alive but were not able to visit or bring them home. They are in the Tanzania camp with the same militia. Some of them had been sexually molested and we ask the United Nations to help us to take children home and be free.

In 1998, a genocide in a city called Kalemie where eighty-nine people were killed at a time. Eighty students and other people who were visitors who were doing business in town. They killed them, they used fire on tires, put gas on tires and burned the people.

In 1998, June 15th, I was in a city called Katanga. We were attacked by the government. Many people were killed and other people went to jail and spent one to one and a half years in jail. At this time we decided to leave the country and go to different refugee camp like Burundi, Rwanda, Kenya, and Uganda refugee camps. Which means, our people are suffering with medical issues, no food, no water, and no clothing.

In my family we have nine children. I have only six in South Dakota. Three children are left in refugee camps in Rwanda and Uganda.

In my own family, there are thirteen siblings. One brother was killed in genocide mentioned earlier. He left his brother's wife and children who are in Burundi refugee camp. They all need assistance. If the United Nations could bring us to the United States, then we need to bring those who are suffering.

My son Laurent, I thank God with a good heart to let all American people read and know about us, the Banyamulenge tribe, and how many many years of suffering without any freedom.

Name: Nkomezi Rumenera

My name is Nkomezi Rumenera and I was baptized in 1994, but I was only baptized without change. I thought it was fun to be baptized, but in September 12th, 1997 that was the day I cannot forget, God came into my heart and I was saved.

We were against other tribes in Congo without any reason, only because we were Tutsi. In 2004, we left the country, we went to Burundi refugee camp. After a few months, I decide to go to Kenya refugee camp. God is good, because we left Burundi, many friends and relatives were killed.

My suggestion is Democratic Republic of Congo can give the Banyamulenge freedom and recognize their citizenship. We have mostly four hundred years in the Congo as other Congolese. Please if the United States could help those who are suffering in other refugee camps.

Name: Esaie Ndayisaba

My name is Esaie Ndayisaba and I was born May 4th, 1979 in the Congo. I was from a Christian family. My parents died in 1998, I was nine years old. We have seven children, two girls, and five boys. We are being raised in hard times. One of my brothers was responsible for us after my parents died.

Many years we are raised and leave in discrimination. I am a Munyamulenge. Our neighbor was Babembe and all the time what was said that we were not a citizen. They said, "you are a Tutsi! That is why we cannot recognize you as a citizen." It was hard for us even in elementary school, it was the same problem because we were not a citizen.

In 1996, it was a war, and we left our village called the Chakira to go to Minembwe village. We were in a refugee camp at that time without any assistance from the Congo government, or the United Nations. Only a few friends would feed us. That time we didn't know, to have only food, and clothes, but we did not have any respect as a human being. No radio said anything about us, and no newspaper reported on us. In those hard times we had, I cannot forget one night.

It was October 1996, two militia come into my house, shoot guns, torture, and terrorize us. We did nothing, it was darkness to us. The same night many people were captured and others were badly wounded. From that time, because I see it all happen. My heart was broken because the violence in our tribe on the children, women, men, and in the presence of many people. The rape, torture, burning and killing is in front for all to see.

In 2001, I was left to go to Burundi refugee camp and I stay for a while. In 2004, our refugee camp was attacked. It was August 13th, 2004, 164 people were killed that night and others badly wounded and burned by fire. The United Nations decided to take them to the United States. We thank you for that and we still have survivors of the Banyamulenge tribe that are in a bad situation. Still in Burundi! If they can get a chance to bring them to the United States to be treated and have freedom and right to have school, food, and employment positions!

I would call the high international courts to bring to their attention to the people responsible for the genocide in Burundi refugee camp. Thank you for letting the people know about the discrimination to the Banyamulenge tribe.

Name: Obedi Rutandara Bukuru

My name is Obedi Rutandara Bukuru and I was born in 1959, in the village of Uvira where there is a small mountain called Bijombo. I now live in Austin, Texas. I live with my eight children. I was baptized in 1975. I was completely changed and saved.

In 1998, my testimony started when we left the country, because of some political issues and the war. I remember it was on a Saturday, in a small town. They said everyone had to be arrested, but it was especially for one tribe. People started to run to the border of Burundi, but it was too late.

They took all the women, men, and children and put them each in three separate schools. They would say, "Today you guys have to be killed!" Our God is good, most of the people were captive for a week then released. Only a few were shot and killed. We start to walk about one hundred miles from Vyura to Kalemie. It was a long way, we lost some children and older people.

In 2002, once in Uvira, people left country to go to Bujumbura camp. We stay there two months, then we decide to go back to the Congo. After some time we left again. We came to Gatumba refugee camp and our family stayed. In August 13th, 2004, it was 9:30pm, and I heard a gun. Then, my children asked," what happened?" "Maybe they come to steal a cow." After a few minutes, there were so many guns firing and the children say, "This is not normal." I decided to go out to see. Once, I went out and I saw some shelters burned, then people were shot. We say, "Lord, Lord, Lord save us, help us!" I come back into my shelter to wake up my family. Once I come in, "they shot my shelter!" Three women and four children were shot and killed, but my family, nobody had been shot. That was good for my family. The older people were killed in my tribe. God protected us on the hand of enemies.

I still have one child in the Bugamboro refugee camp, but eight are with me now. I need to join them in Texas, if possible. I am working, my life changed and my children are in school right now. I can buy whatever I want and my children have access to go to school. I wish older people in refugee camp can have what I have now.

Name: Chantal Ngineri

My name is Chantal Ngineri and I was born July 7th, 1990 in the village of Uvira. I am a Christian, but I was not baptized. In my family there are ten of us, two parents and eight children. We are not all together because some of our family did not pass the interview.

We were living in Uvira and I remember it was June 10th, 2002, the war came to our town. We heard the gun shot and many people started to run toward the border of Bujambora. We went to the refugee camp and stayed about a month. The Burundi government decided to put us in the Gatumba refugee camp. Our tent shelter was a green tent and the rest of the tents were white. The day before the massacre, I was in Burundi hospital with my sister in law. In the evening, we came back to the refugee camp and our shelter was number nine. The time was 9:30 pm, a woman was taking a shower and she saw people. They asked her if she can show the way to the Congo. She said no and was afraid because they were people she did not recognize. She then ran to the back of the shelter. Once she came back, the militia probably already saw the people and started to fire shots. They fired the guns and in thirty minutes, many of the shelters were attacked. That time I saw one child, a girl named Nyampore. She already was shot and she said, "Could you please bind me with a bandage." She was with a boy named Eric, who was shot very bad. They put gas on him and burned him severely. He was crying out, "Please help me!" The people were running in fear and after an hour, he died.

In our shelter, women and children died. The shelter was burning with fire at that time. All the women were shot. We did not have any dead bodies. All was burned. I saw by myself many people who died that night. The next day even in the hospital, people still continue to die.

Now, we need peace and to help those who are suffering in the refugee camp. I am in school and now I have access to education and health. I wish all children who are suffering in refugee camp had access to education, food, and health care.

Name: Neziya Nashinwe

My name is Neziya Nashinwe and I was born in 1969, in the village of Ruzizi, in the Congo. I was baptized but, don't remember the date and time. I was married in 1987.

My life after genocide was very hard, because in 1998, war started in our village. Many people died and some were wounded. I saw many people suffer as well as myself. I was separated from my husband from 1998 to 2005. All the seven years we never saw each other. My husband spent two years in jail and afterward the United Nations took him to the United States. It was a hard time for my husband because he needed to go to school in Texas. He could not fill out the paperwork to tell officials that he left his family in Africa. It was a long hard process.

In 2005, I came to Texas with my children. It was hard time in my life to raise children in the refugee camp without both parents and my husband. All five of my children were little. Now, I am glad to be in the United States. I have access to everything and even being old, I still have a chance to learn.

Please if possible, we need your help to bring all our families together.

Name: Rubin Mazimano

My name is Rubin Mazimano and I was born in the Congo in 1986. I was baptized in Burundi. I am from a small tribe, the Banyamulenge. In my young age, I did not have fun because of so many political issues. We even had trouble in school and outside in the village.

I went to jail in 1998 with my parents and all my siblings. My friends and relatives had been killed the same year in jail. I can't understand why we are in jail for thirteen months. Later, one day, or one month we found out we are same tribe in jail. Then, we ask many questions about being in jail. Why? Explain to us why? The same year I lost two brothers younger than me in jail.

As a student, in Missouri, at Columbus College, I wish this could all come to an end. There are so many people in the refugee camp. There is no food, freedom, or any health care.

I wish that many people in the camp would have a place to live and placement in other countries. I would want all to come together. The children can go to school and a place to sleep without any worries.

We wish freedom and peace for all. I wish this book can be read by many people, college people, and people who have a heart to help.

Name: Yvonne Nyampore

My name is Yvonne Nyampore and I was born January 1st, 1988 in the Congo, in Uvira. I was baptized in 2005, in Bujumbura at a young age. I am with my family of six children and mother. Our father was killed in the Congo.

In August 13th, 2004, it was around 9pm, and I was in our shelter. I went to bed early. I was asleep and heard a voice. I thought it was a dream at first. Someone tell me, "wake up!" I woke up, someone threw a rock and hit my right shoulder. I run and tell my mom, "someone hit me with a stone." Mom had asked me where and I told her my shoulder. Mom checked me and she said to go back to sleep. It was a dream, nothing! That time I felt pain in my shoulder, but really was nothing, a dream. Thirty minutes after we heard people cry. People started to run, we were being attacked in our camp. Mom and others woke up, we were under attack. Two minutes later, I was shot in my right shoulder. I thought it was a dream, but it was not. Earlier, in dream, was that same side. We try to run outside, but it was too late. Many people killed from being wounded, or by fire. That same night they took me to the hospital and I spend two months at Bujambura Hospital in pain. We had a harder time in Gutumba refugee camp.

I wish the United States would help those in need, especially the people in Burundi refugee camp. They need help! I thank God for this book. This will make many people know about the problem with my tribe.

Name: Esperance N. Budutira

My name is Esperance Nyanduhura and I was born September 15th, 1990 in the Congo. In 2006, I was baptized in Rwanda. My family has seven children and both parents, from the time I was baptized. I was changed and I received Jesus Christ as my savior. I cannot remember when we went to Nairobi refugee camp. We had a hard time, a hard life, without food. We never went to school. I was very hard for us to eat ever. Simple meal, but our God never leave us alone. God provided day by day. We could even spend night, but was not sure if we would have food for the next day.

Now, for me and my siblings, God picked us from many people in our refugee camp to come to the United States. This is the place where we can eat, go to school, have clothes, and find part time job. Our lives were changed totally. We lived without hope, but now we have hope.

Please, if people in the United States get a chance to read this book, they can have a heart to help the refugee camps. God Bless You!

Name: Pastor Nene Rwenyaguza

My name is Pastor Nene Rwenyaguza and I was born in the Congo, in Uvira. My local village was in Katanga. My birth date was January 1st, 1973. I was baptized in 1986.

The same time my life has been changed, but I was called in 1992. I heard a voice call me, "wake up!" and do my work. My testimony is about the war in 1998 to 2003. My village had been attacked so many times by militia. I saw so many people die in front of me. For example, Awigina and Foma died in front of me.

My house had been burned by fire and I was separated from my family. This was the time I was sick and I could not find a hospital. I went to Bujambura refugee camp and stayed there almost one year. Afterward, I decided to go to Nairobi refugee camp. It was not easy to leave the refugee camp because you have to spend one to three years there for protection. The paperwork was given to the government officials and then we have access to have food and medicine. After three years, I found out my family was still alive, but it was in last minute to come to the United States. Then, I cannot go back to the Congo to see them. I decide to come by myself. I left my wife and three children. My wife now has an orphan, which happens when parents are killed. Also, my mother is with the family. Right now, they live in Nairobi. Good news came and the United States gave permission to join me in Missouri. I will not know the day they come, but God is good! I want my family with me again. It has been six years and it is September. I wish that the United States will help our difficult life. God Bless You!

Name: Chantal Mutirabura

My name is Chantal Mutirabura and I was born in the Congo in 1995. Now, I am in a refugee camp in Uganda. There were twelve children in my family. Two were killed in the Congo at the start of 1996. I was a year old, and I had not been in my village home. I was separated from my family because they were in a refugee camp in Rwanda. When I wanted to come join them, hard times hit in the refugee camp. Why can't I join them with the same life?

I am separated from my family. I do not have access to go to school, or go to the hospital when I get sick. I do not know my future. I have almost spent fifteen years in the refugee camp. Please if only some country can have compassion to bring us freedom from the refugee camp. Please help me and help others in my situation. God Bless You!

Name: Tite Nyamushemwa

My name is Tite Nyamushemwa and I was born October 8th, 1964 and was baptized in 1979, in the Congo. Me and my wife have seven children and we now live in Texas.

Since I was selling cows, for many years, I used to have money. One day, it was Saturday, and someone come where we were selling cows. He told us, "Your village is under attack. You are making money, but you have to make sure you cannot be seen by your family any more." After an hour passed, we saw the militia and they told us," If you want to live, give all your money you have to me! All the money!" Then, we see more militia and they told us to take all our clothes off. We were naked and then they tried to find money. The time we were beaten, tortured, and then taken to jail naked. We spent thirty days in jail without food, water, and some of our friends died in jail. Can you imagine thirty days without food, water, and beaten and tortured every morning and evening? It was hard time to try to explain to people how we were treated. After thirty days, they took us out. They said the United States knows people are suffering in jail. They decided to move us from the small jail to a big jail where there were so many people inside.

In the big jail, a doctor was in the jail. He saw us and said, "Since you have not eaten for thirty days, your stomach is small. You must try to eat small amounts of a sauce till your stomach gets bigger and ready to eat." We stayed in same jail for thirteen months. So many people die by being beaten and tortured. It was terrible and after a while, when we began to eat, we realized we were naked. People started to give us clothing to cover up. So many many people!

I was separated from my family for seven years and six months without seeing each other. We went through hard times. I can't believe my wife and children are still alive.

Once, I get to Texas, I was trying to call my family. I would ask if this is my wife on the phone. Voice was changed, and children are grown. The children would ask Mom that maybe they don't have a Dad. I found a job in Texas and I found peace. When I thought about my family, I would not eat, or sleep.

I wish the United States can help others who are in need of help. We do need help from this situation.

Name: Rusi Nyiramahoro

My name is Rusi Nyiramahoro and I was born in the Congo in September 9th, 1983. I was baptized in 1990 in the Congo. In1989, I received the Holy Spirit into my heart. I was younger, God put something in my heart. I start listening for the voice from God. From 1998 to 2002, we left Uvira mountain with peace and without problem. The time we heard a group of militia come into our village and attack our own village, many people were killed, shot down and burned.

In 2002, I remember so clearly, I was in school, in Uvira. One evening, we were surrounded by militia. In town, they said, "We have to kill every Banyamulenge!" It was very hard for us to hear that, but in a few hours be killed. Many people were killed that same night. I witnessed a lady raped, tortured, and violated. From that time, the survival with problems of HIV, Aides, Trauma, is ongoing with a huge need for treatment and counseling. Some of the people are in different refugee camps and others are struggling in the Congo.

I live in Rwanda refugee camp. I am by myself and my siblings are still in the Congo. This is my fifth year without seeing each other as a family. I wish if this book comes out that it can help those who are struggling in different areas.

Name: Patient Murangwa

My name is Patient Murangwa and I was born in 1994 in the Congo at Uvira mountain. I am not baptized yet, and now I am in Nairobi refugee camp.

We lived in a village and one night we heard a gun shot. This was in the middle of the night when nobody could be seen. The people tried to run and flew out of the village to save there own life. From that time, I was separated from my parents. The people told my parents that I was killed. We spent ten to fifteen days in the forest without food or drink. After a while, we decided to go to Burundi refugee camp for safety. We stayed there for one year. We could not find peace and life was hard. We went to Kenya to apply for protection which is a paper that gives permission to go to place of safety. The HCR requires this paper to go to the United States or any other country for safety.

It is not easy to live without parents. I am sixteen years old and I never had any protection in Nairobi. I am still on a waiting list without protection, no access to food, medicine, school, or the paperwork for HCR. Now, my life is stuck in waiting.

I wish that I can find peace and the right to have access to education as other children. Then, I wish one day, I can find where I can live with peace.

Name: Claude Rwaganje

My name is Claude Rwaganje and I was born in 1966 and baptized in 1980. I changed completely because after the baptism I became a new person with new commitment and new ideas. I committed myself to the Lord and became more responsible.

I was in the United States, when all the wars of 1998, 2000, 2002, and the Gatumba massacre of 2004. In 2005, I was able to travel to Burundi and met with several of the Gatumba survivors and also went to visit the massacre site. I will say that the life after the massacre hasn't changed much because many survivors are still in refugee camp without hope. Some of them wanted to return home last year but they were not allowed to enter DRCongo.

Many of the orphanages are still struggling for food, shelter and other primary needs. People are still depressed and need some counseling.

My family is not together. Some of my relatives are still in DRCongo, Burundi, and Rwanda.

I have done different kinds of work from Manufacturing to Accounting. Currently, I am the Executive Director of Community Financial Literacy and organization that I founded in late 2008 which is aimed at training Refugee and New Immigrant communities on basic finance. They will be able to understand how the American Financial System works from banking, savings, investing, and building credit. I figure out that this is the best way to help my fellow refugees who might need this service.

Name: Elizabeth Ngombwa (Laurent's Mother)

My name is Elizabeth Ngombwa and I was born in the Congo village called Rubuja in 1940. I was baptized in 1951 at the Pentecost church, the time I have been saved and received Jesus as my personal savior. This was after my marriage. I have ten children, but three of them have passed away. Two of them were killed in genocide in the Congo, but other one passed away due to sickness, without treatment, no hospital, no food, and no water.

What I can say about life, we had a hard time in our life. God called us when we were young, but to save in our area, there was no reason in the fifties. That time everybody practiced pagan beliefs, witch craft, but because of commitment to be saved by the Lord and do his work we had good things. We saw many people repent, be baptized, and receive salvation from sickness.

I can say 1965, the day I cannot forget in my life. One morning, my children went outside to play with other children. The militia surrounded the village and our children were held captive for five years. This was not only my children, but others. But, now with my children from that time until 1970, I was crying. I lost hope, I can't even have happiness time in my life. Can you imagine to have three children, one was eleven, another seven and the other five who were held captive by militia. We did not know if they were alive or dead. Can you think how I felt?

God is good, after five years God brought all my children home alive. I cannot forget to let other parents who lost their children how they felt. I see the sorrow in their heart. This was the same sorrow I felt before my children came back home.

I thank my husband from the time he told me even our children are captive. God told me in my heart they are going to come back alive. Once I was crying, he encouraged me that I will see them again. I think any of the Banyamulenge tribe, my husband is one who has a strong faith and this can be testified by many people in our tribe. Why, I say this is because my husband did not stop giving them the gospel everywhere he was preaching. He had the confidence that our children will come back.

I thank you for our neighbor from the time our children were captive. We received neighbors to visit, pray with us, and give a message of encouragement. I think of the three children who went into the forest and were held captive for five years without love, and compassion of parents for all the things they had experienced in their lives. I thank them for their patience.

I thank you my son in law and daughter in law in supporting me in my time of need. I definitely thank you Laurent as my last born and Debbie Heagy because this book will make many people know what has happened in our lives in the Congo, not only my family but for all the tribe. My husband, even this book can come out even when we pass away we know our history can read forever.

I thank God for the faithful and goodness for my family.

Name: Issac Sebaganwa

My name is Issac and I was born in 1933 in the Congo, in the village of Mulenga. I was baptized in 1954, I cannot remember the day or month. I thank Pastor Zachary who helped me to become Christian. I was seen without Jesus, but he helped me a lot. My own children are seven in total. Two have been killed in genocide in the Congo and the last two were killed in a refugee camp in Burundi. We had so many hard problems against our tribe. So so many people has been killed from 1965 till now in the Congo.

In 1998, our village was attacked by militia and the Congo government. People were killed and burned. The women were raped and the children killed by Machete

We left the country from that time to look where we can find peace.

In 2003, we went to Burundi refugee camp to hopefully find peace. We stayed there about one year. At 10pm, I was not asleep and I felt heavy in my heart that evening and did not eat. My wife gave me something to eat but was unable to eat. I mentioned to my wife how I felt. I was not sick. In a few minutes, I heard guns and I told people to run. They said," no, because people want to steal." After ten minutes, my shelter is being attacked. Three people were killed at that time, my daughter in law was shot in the stomach. She stated," Could you please take my children out, because I am dieing." I told her, "How can I leave you after you were shot?" She said, "I am already dead, go with my children." I went outside with my grandson out back. Once out of tent, I saw a man named Ntoni who was shot in the chest and head. He was bleeding and said, "Issac please could you give me a hand to get up." I had my grandson who was shot. He pleaded for help to give him a hand. I gave him my left hand, then he was able to get up and run. We ran together, but he was shot bad. Once we get somewhere, he never wake up. He was in a coma for two months at the hospital. He is still in Burundi refugee camp still struggling. Interviews were starting while he was in a coma, to leave and he did not get interviewed. The case is done. Please, I hope this book will help him come to the United States.

The next morning, I found my daughter in law. She was shot, but still alive. We are with her in South Dakota. She has two children here and the rest of her children are still in Burundi. We hope one day they can join us in South Dakota. Thank you for letting the American people know what is happening in our tribe.

Name: Laurent R. Munyamahoro

My name is Laurent R. Munyamahoro and I was born August 18th, 1976. I was baptized in the Congo, in 1992. I accepted Jesus Christ as my Savior and was committed to leaving the scene and to become a new creation. My life was changed by making a covenant with Jesus that he will lead and guide my life.

My life was really bad after genocide in the Congo. I see so many people the same age being killed. I saw the children, men, and women who have been raped and violated. So many refugee people run away from our village to seek peace which means now. The people are located in different refugee camps in different countries. Many wounded and so many casualties. The people without limbs struggle in their life. So many people have HIV Aides and no treatment given out to them. The children at a young age with HIV and mothers with HIV bearing children with HIV Aides. There is some held captive now who don't know if any relatives are alive or dead who are in the camps. It's a big problem that our tribe is against many other tribes. Our tribe is a target.

I am not with all my family. Some are in the Congo and others are in the refugee camp in Burundi. Once we need unification of our family, then peace. Thank you very much.

Name: Etienne Ngenda Bizimans

My name is Etienne Ngenda Bizimans and I was born in the Congo, in 1977, a place called Kabara Uvira.

Before their displacement, the Banyamulenge Tutsi, were pastoralist living in the plateau region of South Kivu Province in eastern Congo. They are devout Christians and speak Kinyamullenge, a language closely related to Kinyarwaada and Kirundi, the national language of Rwanda and Burundi respectively.

Before the Congo gained independence in 1960, relations between the Banyamulenge and their neighbors were usually peaceful. They occasionally fought with tension over the land use. In the mid 1960's during the Samba rebellion that broke out in the Southern Congo. During that rebellion, my Grandfather Kirayi went to captivity for two months and my families were forced to flee their homes and village for towns such as Uvira. Therefore, the first time many were exposed to the enmities of modern life acquired a thirst for education that persists unto this day. They were not able to return home, that caused so many deaths, disease, and malnutrition.

During the wars and massacres, for our village many militia from everywhere, come in our village and take Banyamulenge's riches like cows, goats, sheep, and nobody could follow them for fear of getting shot.

In the 1996 war, so many Banyamulenge had hard time, so many families were murdered, famine, disease, sorrow, and general breakdown of social order. The families were broken, separated, mutilated, and many of us were taken into captivity. We have been tortured up to now, and there was a general desperation and hopelessness so everyone fled to wherever he or she find safety. That is why so many of the refugees are in different refugee camps suffering and dieing. The trouble caused many of us to flee our native land and go around the world searching where we can find peace.

A thousand of us went to Burundi where hundreds of the Banyamulenge were killed, burnt in their shelter in Gatumba and other refugee camps. The survivors who were injured badly resettled in the United States and other countries. The remaining people are still suffering by the government and other organizations.

I am separated from my wife and children. This is the third year we have not seen each other. I have hope the paperwork is in the process.

The rehabilitation and counseling center should be made available for all people who have been traumatized. Justice and human rights to be guaranteed to each and everyone. We need to create security guards for the Banyamulenge tribe. We need to promote Christianity all over again, build churches, worship centers, preach repentance, forgiveness and reconciliation. We need to build hospitals where people have access to health care. God Bless You!

Name: Esther Namahoro Bukuru

My name is Esther Namahoro Bukuru and I was born January 1st, 1978 in the Congo. I was baptized in 1993 in the village of Minembwe. Before I was baptized, I had been changed by myself in 1992. I heard a voice in me and I felt my life was changed.

In the year 2000, it was around 4am, one man woke up and went around our village. He was traveling to the next village. Once he walked about one mile, he saw people and he asked them who they were. They did not respond. He asked two times, then he ran. Once he ran back to the village, he was shot. It was night and there were many trees, they did not kill him. Then he ran in village and woke up everyone. He stated that they are being attacked by the militia. If others heard it they would go tell another neighborhood. It took longer and the village was under attack. They killed two people and two homes were burned. At this time, I was separated from my husband. I did not know if he was held captive or killed. We have been separated for four years. Then, they told me in Burundi refugee camp, he was there. Then, after three months, they said he went to Tanzania refugee camp, but I cannot believe he was still alive. There was no communication until 2007, I decide to go myself to see if I see him in the refugee camp in Tanzania. I was with my two boys when we went to the refugee camp in Bujambura. We stayed two months because it is dangerous to travel by myself. I am not able to speak another language. Then I had sorrow in my heart being separated from my husband. One day I decided to travel to Tanzania. We found people with a bicycle taxi and we paid a little money to travel. They took us to the river and we paid money to ride the boat. The boat took us to the refugee camp Nyarugus which is in Tanzania. It took us twelve hours to get there. Can you imagine traveling in a bicycle taxi and boat for twelve hours? Some hills we had to walk up where the bicycle taxi could not go up with people in the taxi. Once we arrived at the refugee camp the United Nations and HCR asked me if I was for sure from the Congo. I told them yes, and they asked me if it was possible to show a picture that I could recognize him? They asked me the full name and his birth date. I told them and they took me to another refugee camp. I started the interview process. Then, one evening they brought the picture. They asked me if this was my husband? I said yes and then, they worked on the paperwork. It took one month and then they took me back to see my husband.

I had a hard time. Once in Tanzania, I was pregnant with a girl, and I had my two boys with me. It was not easy to stay there at the refugee camp for two years. But, God is good. I live in Dayton, Ohio with my husband and three children.

Name: Paul Mukiza

My name is Paul Mukiza and I was born in 1960, in the Congo. I have a wife and four children. My own village was named Rubumbasha.

We were in the market one evening selling cows. Some of our friends who was also selling cows told me about an announcement on the radio. The announcement said, "Kill every Banyamulenge that is in the area." In one hour, our friend was arrested, beaten, and killed. We were trying to see where we can run. One man who was our friend took me with other people. We were together and they put us on the top of his house. We stayed there for three months and eight days. We did not go outside and was provided something to eat. The Congolese people told the militia that this household has Banyamulenge inside. By night, the militia come in the house and told the man that they were here for an investigation. They take out everyone who was inside the house and take us all to the big jail called Bakita. I saw so many people there. The same jail I found my wife and other people. I spent ten months in Bakita. People were tortured and killed. Every single night the army would surround the jail, take two to five people out to be killed and never seen again.

One day we saw the Red Cross come in the jail. They told us to not be afraid because the United Nations knows how the Congo government treated and killed our people. They said, "From now on, no one will be killed." Can you think how one hundred and twenty one people can be in a small room in the jail for ten months. We could not sit down or sleep. There was only one small toilet we all used in the jail. We spent six months without seeing our children who were also in this same jail. It was a tough time.

In Bakita jail, one man died with cancer, and another with a heart attack. But, myself I could not see well, because my eyes are bad. I stayed in the dark all the time. I also had problems with my ears in jail.

In the other jail, so many people were killed and we don't have too much information for them. We are not sure if anyone survived.

I used to have a big farm and all the cows, goats, and sheep were killed. They took all of my land. I am separated from the children because of the war. I took care of a brother to a relative and he died. Then, I took care of a child. My brothers are in refugee camps of Burundi in Rwanda, and Tanzania.

Name: Innocent Rwiyereka

My name is Innocent Rwiyereka. I was born January 1st, 1997 in the Congo, in the village called Kinyoni. I was baptized without change. In 2006, when I was in the refugee camp, I received Jesus Christ as my Lord and Savior. I felt like I was washed with water. It was a sign of forgiveness of my sin.

In 1998, my village was attacked by the militia and people were killed. Now, the Congo still has trouble as you read on the Internet, or listen on the radio. In 2000, my village was attacked again and I was separated from my family at the time. I went to the refugee camp in Rwanda, Burundi. I found peace there.

In 2004, I decided to go to Tanzania refugee camp. I was with a friend. It was hard for us to travel from Burundi to Tanzania without any money or anything. Once we get to Tanzania, we found other refugees from the Congo, but they were those who are against our tribe. The United Nations and HCR told us that they are not seeking refugees, but the army which was not true. They were going to kill the army. We had so many interviews without argument of being refugees in camp. They transferred us to another camp in Imbuba refugee camp. We stayed there several months, then they transferred us to another refugee camp named Nyarugusu. We spent many many days without food, and can't have any freedom like the other refugees. Everybody was new and we were Banyamulenge. It was a tough time in our life, but one day God brought us out of there. Now, I am in Dayton, Ohio with my family.

I am not with all my family because my mom and nephew are still in a refugee camp. My mom and nephew are alive and they are in the Kenya refugee camp. I would like my mom and nephew to come to Dayton, Ohio where I am now living.

Name: Charles Rumenge

My name is Charles Rumenge and I was born in 1984 in the village of Vyura. I was baptized in 1996, but I cannot remember the date. There is no certificate at present time. I did change and I decided myself to follow Jesus Christ after being saved. I was transformed, because I thought being saved was normal and at that time I knew so many things. I recognize that God protected me from so many people who were killed, burned, and wounded.

In 1998, there was a war in my village. This war was against my tribe because other tribes said to kill Banyamulenge. So many people left the village and others left the country. One leader named Ndombasa Herodando gave a speech. He said, "kill every Banyamulenge and everyone who looks like him." From that time we never had peace, but for myself, we left the Congo and moved to Burundi. Then, in 2004, we had a genocide in the refugee camp and I was separated from my parent at that time. I went to Tanzania refugee camp until now and I never see them again in six years. Let me say a little about Tanzania refugee camp, because I spent most of my time there for six years. We had discrimination and we struggled because we were poor, no food, no drink, or clothes. Other refugees were against us and we never had freedom as other refugees. Somehow, the UNHCR tried their best to protect us from other tribes. There was so many problems that we never had a permanent refugee camp. We were moved around to other refugee camps and this was not safe.

The UNHCR tried their best to do the paperwork and interviews to get the chance to become a citizen on the United States. Now, I am in Dayton, Ohio and I thank God for this. I am at peace. I have freedom. I can go to any school or college and find any kind of work. I wish all Banyamulenge who are struggling in different refugee camps can find peace, education, and health.

Name: Aimable Nkundabantu

My name is Aimable Nkundabantu and I was born in the Congo, in 1994. I am an orphan. I lost both parent in genocide. Now, I am in Nairobi refugee camp. I am trying to see if I can get protection and start process to go to United States or other country for peace. I have had a hard time leaving Nairobi without food, and medicine. I only wish I can have freedom and access to education and sponsorship. Thank You

Name: Aimee Kinyana

My name is Aimee Kinyana and I was born in 1991 in Uvira, Congo. I was baptized in 2006 and from that time I was changed. We had so many problems because some of the people left the country to go seek peace.

The family is separated. The children lost their parent. Now, I spend three years in Nairobi, but I was not recognized as a refugee. I do not have access or benefits in Nairobi and I was separated from my parents in Uvira till now. I do not know if they are still alive or have passed away. I don't have access to education, medicine, or anything. People in Nairobi are hopeless. We wish people can understand our stories and testimonials and they can help us. Thank you very much in letting other people know our problem.

Name: Pastor Moise Sebahizi

My name is Pastor Moise Sebahizi and I was born in 1947, in a village called Ruvumera which is in the Uvira district. I was baptized in 1954, in Romera. I was baptized in a river. I was changed before being baptized. Our local spiritual leader told us to choose one name for the baptism. I choose Aron. When I was asleep in the night, someone came into the dream, a man. He stated, "you choose your own name, but I want to give you a powerful name Moise." From that time, I have been in a good relationship with God up to the present.

I was leaving the Bijombo area in 1998. War come in our village. We have been attacked by militia. Some of the troop was on the government side and so many people were killed that time. We left our village, we walked ten days on foot until we came to Uvira city. We stayed there until 2002. The war came again in Uvira and all kind of hatred was against our tribe. We left to go to Bujambora refugee camp. The militia came again in 2004 and they attacked in Bujambora refugee camp. God protected me and I never lost anyone in my family at that time, but in the Congo, I lost one. They say my son died, but I have not seen my son's body.

Thirty years ago, I had a dream and God told me, "you all are going to die until I take you to the United States." This was the first time I heard United States in my dream. This was God's promise.

I do not have work, but I serve God in Nazarene Church in San Diego, California. A person my age cannot go into manufacturing work. One of our children is in Nairobi refugee camp. We wish if all people are struggling in camp to have help and support. God Bless this vision to let Americans know about us in this book.

Name: Zera Nakanimba (Wife of Pastor Moise Sebahizi)

My name is Zera Nakanimba and I was born in 1948. I am sixty-two years old and I was born in village of Bijombo in Uvira District. I had seven children, but I lost one son. We knew he died in war, but did not see. I was baptized when I was twelve. My Mother used to be an Evangelist in our village. Then, she died from a disease due to no access to hospital. My Mother died in 1966. She gave me a legacy to obey God.

In 1965, we used to live in village called Gatongo. One evening, my husband and I felt something was wrong, but did not know. My husband told me that we will leave the village together. The day after we leave the village, the militia attacked the village. There were twelve families and all were killed and burned by fire. God is good, he protected us.

In 2004, in Gatumba refugee camp in Bujambura, one week before genocide, we see someone come in our shelter. He said, "I want to pay rent for your place, then you can leave the shelter and live in small city." Then, one week after, the refugee camp was attacked. So many people died, they were shot and burned.

If I remember how God protected us through so many genocides, I am humble and I praise the Lord. I wish to help all people still in refugee camp.

Name: Justin Nsenga, M.S.

My name is Justin Nsenga and I was born in 1974 in the DRC, the then Zaire in Minembwe territory in the village of Ilundu. My family moved from Minembwe to Bibogobogo when I was about six years old. I was baptized in 1992 at the age of eighteen years old. I was born and grew up pretty much in a saved family. Both of my parents were saved and served the Lord since they were young to the present time. My baptism was a confirmation or transition from being a young Christian to a full man ready to serve God. In my local church, it was a tradition that no one could participate at the Lord's table before getting baptized. After my baptism, I was able to participate with other members of my church. I was a choir member before I was baptized and I continued to serve in that ministry until 2005. After being baptized, I was initiated to the other area of the church ministry such as preaching, praying in the church, or serve in other ministries in my local church.

My life has been a daily struggle since 1994 when I left my family behind to go to Rwanda. At this time, it was a choice between life and death. Soon after the Rwandan genocide, my tribe became a real target not only of the Zaire soldiers, but also Hutu refugees from Burundi, or Rwanda. In 1993, I remember when my colleagues and I were jailed for six hours in Uvira by the government soldiers just because we were Tutsi. I and my friends were accused of killing the President of Burundi, Mr. Ndadaye Melchior. The astonishing part of this is that I had never been in Burundi even for one day. I was merely a simple student in Uvira, just a few miles from Burundi. I wasn't a politician or having anything to do with what happened in Burundi. I had nothing to do with what happened in Rwanda (the war between the RPF and the Government of Kigali). Just a few months after that episode and others that were similar, we realized that it was not safe for me to stay in the Congo. It was a very hard and difficult decision for my family and I to separate. My last time of living with my parents was in September 1994. Ever since, I have lived a life on my own, but God has been on my side and I now enjoy being alive despite all the hardships I went through.

1996-2008 War: I was far from my family, but never had peace in my heart. My family had to flee from the place where we lived to a "safe" place. My siblings and parents had to walk hundreds of miles under the rain, without any food just to save their lives. During that period, hundreds of people were killed. Every Munyamulenge was in danger wherever he/she was in the Congo. The killings occurred as if it were planned. Hundreds of families were separated from their loved ones, kids, senior people were ruthlessly massacred, the villages were burned down. I was attending a School of Journalism in Rwanda, but during that year, my life was difficult. I couldn't focus on my studies, every evening we, I and other Banyamulenge students, would gather in a room to listen to the radio about the war in our country the DRCongo. Many of my colleagues lost their parents during the war. It was difficult to console one another. However, we never forgot to pray for our parents and for our siblings and for the entire country that was in war. Personally, I remember one evening a friend of mine came to me and told me that my family (my mother, and my young siblings) had been wedged in a war zone, and that my young brother was killed in Uvira town along with many other people. It was even hard for me to cry. I was numb; I couldn't even have courage to pray. I silently prayed deep inside of my heart asking God why all that was happening to my people. At some point, I felt like God had turned his back from us. But, I never lost hope that one day we will live in our country again. This I knew, everything happened for us to learn a lesson, to see how great is our God and how we shouldn't hold on to material things. During all these consecutive wars, people have learned to live with less, people have been resilient to live without their families, parents and their children have been separated and scattered around the four corners of the world.

2004 Gatumba Massacre: The massacre of more than a hundred refugees Banyamulenge in Gatumba camp occurred just after two months I arrived in the United States. It was on August 13th 2004 at 2am when I and other young people, and the Apostle Simeon Mukwiza, were in an overnight prayer at the International Christian Fellowship in Portland Maine. One young man among us received a call from Burundi stating that people in refugee camps have been massacred. We took a time to pray and try to stay strong and keep our hope in God. The next morning, I discovered that more than twelve people from my extended family were killed among those others. This was a moment when people became insensible, not that we didn't care, but because we were powerless to make any difference in that moment; all news was bad news; announcing the death of people we know, our brothers, our sisters, and our parents. The next day, the entire world stood up and condemned the atrocities. However, the massacre of these Banyamulenge refugees has been a history, and no one cared then, and now nobody seems to care. Only, God knows what will be our future. After the Gatumba massacre, all the people from the community of Banyamulenge, were discouraged. They feared about their lives because nowhere in the great lakes region was a safe place to live. Now, hundreds of thousands of Banyamulenge are scattered in Burundi, Rwanda, Uganda, and Kenya. I always wonder where our will comes from; our salvation. The only hope we hold on to is our God.

Likewise, other Banyamulenge families, my family is not together. I live in the United States with my wife, our three children, and my sister. My other siblings are in Rwanda and in Uganda, and my parents are still in DRCongo. I work for Catholic Charities Maine as Case Manager.

Name: Rose Mapendo

My name is Rose Mapendo. I am a refugee from the Democratic Republic of Congo, from the Banyamulenge Tutsi tribe. Thank you from the bottom of my heart for giving me this opportunity to tell you my story.

I remember the Tutsi genocide in Rwanda. But, I never thought the same thing could happen in the Congo. All of us were shocked when Tutsi were arrested and executed in all the provinces of Congo. Soldiers took my husband and many other men to be killed. Every night the guards came and took more people to kill them. Every night we thought we would be the next to die.

Then, I found out I was pregnant. I became crazy and very sad thinking how I would survive with the pregnancy and with seven children when I did not have food, water, clothes, or any medical care. It was very hard. I gave birth to twins in prison, a very dirty place that children were using as their bathroom. I used a dirty stick to cut the umbilical cords and I used a piece of hair to tie them. I felt that God showed me to name these boys after the commanders of the death camp-to show those men honor and forgiveness and to let them know I was not their enemy.

My body was the only blanket and diapers my babies had. I was angry and sad and I asked God to let me die before I had to watch my children die. But, I decided to ask God to forgive me of my anger and to forgive my persecutors. After that, I became very strong and free from anger. It gave me strength to live and to encourage my children and the others in the death camp. I felt that I was a new and free person.

While I was in the death camp for sixteen months, I watched the soldiers kill so many people. To keep my heart happy, I used to sing to myself and my children. That song is, "I am hiding in Jesus. He is my refuge. Nothing will take peace from me. No enemy will make me scared. When there is to much sun, He is my shadow. When it is dark, He is my light and protection. When it is raining, He is my umbrella to keep me from getting wet. When the flood comes, it will never take me away. I will never leave where God is. He will never leave me. He is my close friend..."

I can never thank the U.S. Government (Clinton's administration) enough that sent rescue teams and Sasha Chanoff to rescue us. I came here with nine children and one grandchild without a dime, without a house, without medical care, without food. The U.S. Government has helped me raise my children and it is helping them get an education.

When I got here, life was not easy. I am a widow with many children. I could not read or write English. I was very sad. Many of my friends had been killed. My twins spent two months in the hospital because they we sick. I did not know if they would survive. I did not know if my parents were alive.

Many people helped me in America like my brother Kigabo Mbazumutima, my friends, Debra and Toni Lee, and many others. My resettlement agency, Catholic Charities, helped my kids get into school. I found a job taking care of older people. My older children and I work and go to school to support our big family. It has not been easy.

I am a U.S. Citizen now. My twins are nine years old. All my children are in school, including my three oldest who are in college. My oldest son is studying Pharmacy. My oldest daughter is studying Nursing. My second son just graduated from High School. They are all doing well and taking advantage of the opportunities in America.

Now, I have a dream. This dream has two parts. First, I want to be a source of encouragement to widows and orphans from wars in Africa. If I was able to forgive my enemies and to focus on the future, they can do it too.

The second part of my dream is that I want to be a source of help and encouragement for refugees living in America. If I can walk a journey of success, they also can be successful.

I see God's hand in my life. I have survived because God has a purpose for me. God wants me to tell you my story so you can understand the life of a refugee. Thank You

Name: Modeste Kigabo Mbazumutime

My name is Modeste Kigabo Mbazumutime. I am forty-four years old and I was born in the eastern part of the Congo. The high plateau of South Kivu. The village with no road, no electricity, no water, and no access to health care. Women had babies at home. In my family ten were born at home, and Mom had trouble with her last baby. She needed to go to the hospital and it took four to five days to arrive and give birth.

I was baptized in 1982 in expressing publicly my Christian faith. Since my baptism I understood that I need to read the bible and know what God expects from me as a Christian. After my baptism, I did what I could to be faithful to God and my vow to serve him as a Christian follower. There are ups and downs in my Christian life. The path is never straight. God does not have ups and downs, he is always the same and always ready to help me.

Life was normal when people got sick with no treatment. There were wise men and women that would give leaves with medicine to the sick. The sick would either get better or die. People chose to stay at home to die. Many people lived in remote areas where they did not have access to any health care facility. The sick and pregnant women would walk for several days to reach a facility that was poorly equipped. In 1998, the Democratic Republic of Congo lost 5.4 million people due to treatable and preventable diseases.

My older sister achieved her high school diploma and she was my hero. She died while she was giving birth. She would tell me to be smart in school and become the first doctor in our village. I was real serious in wanting to become a doctor. When I made my decision, it was a real challenge for my parents to pay tuition. I did not get assistance from the government. After graduation, there was no tax exemption to assist in my dream to bring health care to my village.

After the genocide, we lost siblings, friends, and relatives. We had to leave our country. We did not have any possibility to return due to the wars that continue along with persecution of Tutsi changes form instead of stopping. There are always new tactics to confuse the international community by using Tutsi, or by associating them to actions that go against them directly or indirectly. In 1994, Rwanda lost one million people in a hundred days, due to genocide.

When I built a clinic with my sister Rose Mapendo, the Arizona State program took my dream to a higher level in finding a way to be a non-profit organization. This would become part of the team to provide a service to the people.

I am President and Chief Executive Officer of Africa Health New Horizons in Arizona. This is a based non-profit organization that brings medical, technical expertise, and facilities to the Great Lakes region of Africa. The donations help fund operation and financial assistance in building the training and health care facilities, transport medical supplies, and provide technology to the Congo, Rwanda, and Burundi.

There are many needs to help the health care facilities to operate smoothly. We need financial support, medical equipment, supplies, human resources, communication resources, phones and computers. We also need Internet service to provide communication between health facilities, health care teams of doctors, nurses, and assistants.

My wife and five children live with me in the United States. Thank You.

Name: Dorcas Nyamukobwa

My name is Dorcas Nyamukobwa and I was born in the Congo in 1950, I was baptized in 1965. I am a Christian and I have changed and received Jesus Christ as my Savior. In my life, I cannot begin to explain my sorrow I have in my heart There has been so many genocides in the Congo. I have escaped death so many times, but our Lord has protected me which I am very thankful. So many people have been killed in front of me. Our men, women, older people, young children, and babies have been killed in horrible ways, I will never forget

I am in the Nairobi refugee camp. I take care of other orphans because they lost their parent. Some are related to me and others are not related. I have a hard life to raise these orphans without assistance. I have been separated from my children for so many years due to war in Congo. I wish I can see them in the United States. We can live together and try to help raise the orphans together. God Bless You and God Bless your work.

Name: Choco Amone Kimazi

My name is Choco Amone Kimazi and I was born in the Congo January 1, 1952. I was baptized in 1970 and it was Christmas Day, December 25th. I was baptized in the river Minembwe, by Pastor Makombe. I have first of all to thank God, the one who has protected me from many deaths. I never went to school, but by now I have a job. I own a house in Portland, Maine. The house has four bedrooms and a nice yard. My life has been improved; from near death in genocide to the point I am able to help other people as much as I can.

I was living in 1998 in the village called Vyura. I decided to go sell a cow in Lubambashi. I remember it was March 15th, 1998. I had a small radio in the evening. Then, someone told me, "Are you listening to the news?" I said, "yes," but I did not understand all that was said because the station was in french. Then after two hours, one of the men who was with me told me, "Don't go anywhere, even to market, because our tribe has been attacked in South Kivu." Then one night a group of the military came and knocked on our house. There was four military men and they said, "Today, give us all your money that you have and you are being arrested today because your tribe tried to go against our Government." It was not true!

The Government attacked our tribe and gave announcement, "Kill everyone in Banyamulenge Tribe!" In speech, many top people said, "Kill Kill Kill!" The military took us, we were beaten, tortured, even some of us were killed that same night. They took us to a small jail, a private jail. We spent a month there without food, water, everything. After one month, some of us died and they decided to take the rest of us to Bakita Jail. They took us without our clothes, we were naked. Once we arrived in Bakita Jail, the women we saw in jail, could not hardly look at us because we were naked, we looked and smelled bad, because we were without food and water. We spent thirteen months in this big jail. We were given small amounts of food here to the point of not being full or we would die. I thank Sofia, she's one who saw me in my situation in jail. She decided to take her five year old daughter Dolla, to have her bring a small amount of food and water. She brought me something to eat and drink every day, because the militia surrounded the jail, they could not suspect the little girl. This is how I survived. My eyes are bad, I spent the time in jail in the dark. I still have problems with my eyes.

I have two of my children who are staying in Nairobi refugee camp. I wish people could come to this country (United States), to see the improvement of life.

God Bless You

Name: Jeremiah Mazimano

My name is Jeremiah Mazimano and I was born in 1946 in Uvira. I have been baptized, but cannot remember the date. I want to thank God who has protected my family. Some of my children, my sons have been killed in Bakita Jail, because of how they looked like Tutsi. My two sons were innocent, I miss them, I love them. As a Christian, I know one day I will see them in heaven.

My life is very good now, because I have my own house in Columbia, Missouri, where all my family live. I wish all Banyamulenge Tribe still struggling in the refugee camps could have access to come to the United States and they could have peace. We remember all the people who have lost their life in the Congo from so many genocides.

God be with them!

Name: Roland Runezerwa

My name is Roland Runezerwa. I was born in a small village called Kabara, in South-Kivu province in Democratic Republic of Congo/ formerly Zaire.

My father Elie Gisaro is a pastor from Methodist Church in the high plateau of Uvira. He was ordained pastor since 1960. His entire career is a firm commitment to serve God. He served the Lord in many parts of the Congo. He was the first man of God to bring good news in Maniema/Kindu Province in the Congo where many tribes were serving the idols without knowing the good news of Jesus Christ. As the first person to bring the Gospel, he told them that there is one God; the maker of Heaven and Earth. He endured many sufferings for the sake of our Lord Jesus during that period; many times they wanted to kill him but the Lord protected him. In my life, I was touched because of my Dad's testimony. Now, he is serving God in South Kivu, he will soon retire from his attributes and responsibilities in his church.

I had a dream of raising a Ministry of Young Missionaries from Central Africa in 2004 when I was at Butare at National University of Rwanda. The aim is to prepare young missionaries who are equipped to bring and to promote the word of the gospel all over the world. Since that time I thought of America, Europe, Australia, Asia as well as Africa where many people are dying in their sins. I immediately called my friend Laurent Muvunyi and shared my vision with him. He advised me to continue keeping my vision (Jeremiah 1:4-10) that I go through prayer. Apart from the vision I shared with my friend Laurent Muvunyi about how we can help vulnerable and disadvantaged people in our tribe and the book he thought of writing many years ago. I thought of some other interventions like: Education (Building a Primary and Secondary School), Health Center in my village and a program of peace and reconciliation in Countries where wars reigned.

In 2007, many times the dream came in my mind that I thought of a way of starting. I realized that the world needs people who are equipped and prepared in order to reach all corners of the planet. In fact, some churches failed to play their roles not because they are not willing to bring the good news, but because people don't have means and tools to meet the spiritual needs.

We have many talented young boys and girls. What they need is the assistance or the follow-up in order to help them out what they are so that they fulfill the great commission written in the Gospel of Mark.

When I was in my second year at the University, many people from my tribe were killed in Gatumba, Burundi simply because of the way they were created. The first time the film was shown at National University of Rwanda, where different people watched the film, a lot of people were traumatized. I remember we stopped our classes, it was hard. From that very day, I said I must serve my people and the rest of the world to fight against discrimination and destabilization of security. These events took place just after a massive displacement of Banyamulenge from Bukavu and Uvira, Bibogobogo, Vyura, Khlemie, and other places.

Events of killings took place in many parts of the Congo where we lost many educated people including the Kamina Camp of Military Officers in Shaba province. Discrimination is the root cause of killings and massacres in the Congo.

This is a testimony about coping with death of four family members from genocide.

Name: Freddy Kaniki

My name is Freddy Kaniki, I was born in a small village called Kamombo in the DR of Congo in a family of 7, 4 brothers and 2 sisters. My father Rev. Jonas Rukema was a pastor in the free Methodist church. We lived in a region with conflicts and hatred between different tribes. My father believed in reconciliation, love and unity, he lived his life for that. We left our community when I was 3 and he started pasturing churches of other tribes in the region. He dreamed of a land of tolerance, he dreamed of love, he dreamed of unity. In my early years I knew I was different from the other kids in the neighborhood, because I was called different names, but I did not know who I was since there was no one from the tribe in the town we lived in. I remember when we returned to south Kivu province from Bunia in 1985, I was 10 and I did not know how to introduce myself the way it is done in my culture: Your name, your Dad's name, your grandfather and your clan. We were completely blended in the different tribes we lived with and we viewed ourselves as one of them. Yet we were perceived as foreigners and sometime enemies. That consideration later intensified when the Congo received refugees from Rwanda after the 1994 genocide, many of them active participants in the mass killing of Tutsi.

In 1995, I decided to go to Rwanda to attend the National University of Rwanda leaving my entire family in the Congo.

On June 23, 1996 I received a letter from my father; he said to me, I quote: "I'm almost sure that we may not see each other again, but be strong and know that our family invested in you, and that family will need to harvest the seed it planted in you one day, I trust you. The Lord I served will be with you." Many times, we asked him to leave that area and cross the run for his life, but he always said he cannot leave the church, for he will never forgive himself if he abandoned the church he was given to pastor.

In September of the year 1996, he was taken with all 3 of my brothers from our house to an undisclosed location; he was later killed on September 22nd with his 3 sons in Kamanyola. The bodies were thrown into the Ruzizi River according to witnesses. At this time of my life, everything became dark with no hope to ever see light again. I felt like I had no reason to live, I had no joy and life did not make sense anymore. For 3 months I could not focus on anything including my studies. I was depressed, hopeless and helpless.

In December 1996, I was becoming useless and I buried all my dreams and ambitions. I then decided to take time to pray, I asked for a room for one week at Gisakura tea plantation in the Nyungwe forest where one of my relatives was a director. I stayed there for a week with a gallon of juice. I did not pray as much as I planned, rather I spent time reading the bible and thinking about what my life was becoming. I was inspired to realize that I could not get my life back as long as I had not forgiven those who killed my family. I had a grudge against them; my mind was full of ill will that was draining me every day. I had no power for revenge, yet I could not let it go. I had attempted to forgive in the past but there was no reason to forgive, whoever did it did not deserve forgiveness. Two things bothered me and were an obstacle to my ability to forgive: The fact that they died not for anything they may have done, but because of who they were, Tutsi; yet no one ever chose to be born in his/her family, it is sad and outrageous that someone should die just because he/she was born Tutsi. Second, my father was betrayed by the very people he trusted, his church members. Especially, when I remember that he could have escaped but chose to stay because of his dedication to the church. Today the church has another pastor, yet I will never get another father.

The reality is we do not forgive someone because he deserves to be forgiven. We do it for our own sake. It is the key to true healing. When I left that room seven days later, I decided to stop mourning, stand up, dust myself off and move on. I was a different person, I had a smile on my face and things started changing. Six months later, I was as ambitious as I used to be. My grades went back to where they were before and I had my life back.

The words he wrote me in his last correspondence became a source of motivation to success. His memory keeps me motivated until today. I left Rwanda in 2002 and moved to the United States. Starting a new life in the U.S. was not easy, but through all the challenges, I had to face, I kept in mind that I had no choice but to succeed. That is what was asked of me. I learned a lesson in everything I went through, to never give up. It is in the darkest sky that the stars are best seen. The darkness will not last forever, and most of all tough times never last, but tough people do. Today, I am happily married to Esther with two sons, David 7, and Jonathan 5. I work as a director of Pharmacy services in a federal hospital. As much as I miss my father, I think he would be more proud of for living my life to the fullest, rather than mourning him forever. He knows I love him.

Pastor Andree Kajabika

Laurent with Pastor Andree - I had a dream
of a book being written

Pastor Pierre Nzamu – One of the oldest
members of the tribe

Orphan headed families

Pastor Zacharie B. Mashavu (Laurent's father)

Elizabeth Ngombwa (Laurent's mother)

The Memorial Gathering of 2009

The memorial gathering took place in Concord, New Hampshire. The massacre at the refugee camp in Burundi occurred August 13 and 14, 2004, at night when everyone was settling down at bedtime. At that time 166 refugees of the Banyamulenge tribe were killed, and close to 200 others were seriously injured in the fateful attack.

The memorial events started in 2007, and this is the first time the reunion/memorial took place in Concord. Donations for the event helped to defray the expense of housing, transportation, and food. The survivors came from Maine, Texas, New York, Arizona, Iowa, Georgia, and Missouri. People from Central Africa and other countries came to this special event.

Pastors from area churches spoke, prayed encouraging words, and shared various verses from the Bible. The Twenty-Third Psalm brought this whole event together with gentle words of calming guidance and encouragement.

Psalm 23 (KJV)

[1]The LORD is my shepherd; I shall not want. [2]He maketh me to lie down in green pastures: he leadeth me beside the still waters. [3]He restoreth my soul: he leadeth me in the paths of righteousness for his name's sake. [4]Yea, though I walk

through the valley of the shadow of death, I will fear no evil: for thou art with me; thy rod and thy staff they comfort me. ⁵Thou preparest a table before me in the presence of mine enemies: thou anointest my head with oil; my cup runneth over. ⁶Surely goodness and mercy shall follow me all the days of my life: and I will dwell in the house of the LORD for ever.

The speakers said the massacre was a planned attack. The witnesses said the groups of armed militia surrounded the tents where the Congolese Banyamulenge lived at Gatumba. They did not touch the other tents housed by other ethnic Burundi. They open-fired their guns on the unarmed innocent men, women, very young children of all ages, and small babies one to two months old. After they used up their ammunition, they used machetes, then poured gasoline and set fire on the helpless injured and the dead. Some were being burned alive and crying out! More than 200 survivors attended the memorial service.

In the auditorium, a video showed the site of where the massacre occurred. There was an outpouring of emotion among the survivors in viewing the children who were killed, the burned bodies, and the tents. The survivors started to cry and scream. When a child was viewed on the video, someone could say, "This is my child."

Dr. Modeste Kigabo said, "That's why there is screaming." Dr. Modeste Kigabo is a refugee from the Congo. He works with an agency to help bring refugees who are victims of the genocide to the United States.

The scenes are still very painfully graphic to the victims of the genocide. The video was stopped, and the pastor led the emotional group of survivors in prayer. Assistants from the event passed out tissue boxes to people in the audience who were crying.

Philipe Mukwiye, who is a survivor, ran into the forest when he heard voices and shooting. "I heard my own children's cries, and I was helpless as I hid behind bushes," he said. He stated further, "Every survivor has their own pain to overcome and their story to share."

The Banyamulenge's history was briefly reviewed, describing how the Banyamulenge have been persecuted in the Central Region of Africa. In the late 1990s genocide entered into the Congo, tearing the country apart and setting violence against the Banyamulenge people.

The list of the refugees killed during the vicious attack was viewed on the screen in front of the audience. The age of the victims ranged from one to two months to the mid-fifties. The massacre lasted two hours and seriously injured 116 people, who will never lose their scars.

Several hundred Banyamulenge were driven from their homeland. They were moved to Burundi, the United Nations refugee camp. These refugees would never be able to go back to their homes for fear of being killed by militia or government soldiers.

Angeline Nyankamirwa stated," We have sorrow in our heart because of what we, the Banyamulenge, have gone through." She mentioned how her husband and three children were killed in the camp. She stated she was lucky because of her Christian faith, and she was selected to come to the United States.

The survivors, their families of young children, and their friends brought the first indicators of the healing which is taking place. Smiles and hugs were freely given and received as the survivors came together.

The organizers of the event urge the survivors to share their stories in a continuing effort to both progress the healing process and inform the world what has happened. Justice for the survivors will not come unless they share their stories and describe those responsible for the massacre. Instead, more tragedy will occur until the militia and others involved are arrested and tried for war crimes.

Oliver Mandevu, President of the Gatumba Refugee Survivors Foundation, stated, "It's a memory that we should use in order to think about what happened . . . from happening again. Whenever you can bring your voice, please try to help us bring these people to trial."

Finally, Rose Mapendo, who is a survivor, keynote speaker, and 2008 Humanitarian of the Year, shared three important points from her own heart. First, we must remember those who passed. Second, "I thank God that I am still alive." Finally, we must tell the world, so other refugees can be rescued. Then people from Africa and America can see the seed that is planted and be grateful for the Gatumba Foundation and Mapendo Association and others who are still seeking justice for the Banyamulenge people.

Rose Mapendo, herself a Munyamulenge, was a survivor from an earlier genocide in Congo. She urges the survivors to have a heart of forgiveness; this helps them to forgive. She states, "If you don't forgive, you cannot do anything for the past, but you can for the future." Rose reminded those gathered that the tribe is still going through challenges.

The Memorial Gathering of 2010

The Memorial Gathering took place at St. Louis University, commemorating the massacre at a refugee camp in Burundi which occurred August 13 and 14, 2004, at night when everyone was getting ready to sleep. One hundred and sixty-six refugees of the Banyamulenge tribe were killed, and 200 others were seriously injured in the fatal attack. The event was sponsored by the Gatumba Refugees Survivors Foundation based in Albany, New York.

Olivier Mandevu, who is President of the Gatumba Refugees Survivors Foundation, received a special certificate of recognition of the Gatumba Memorial from Kasie Starr, the representative of St. Louis, Missouri.

Olivier Mandevu stated, "This is the fourth year the survivors have met to remember the slayings and call for the end of violence throughout the Congo and the region. This Memorial/Gathering is used to bring spiritual and emotional healing."

Pastors from area churches spoke, prayed encouraging words, and shared various verses from the Bible. Several groups shared their songs of praise with the audience. The gathering was designed to encourage the people to share their stories, as doing so was often difficult for them. Prayer and singing helped the people to cope and to heal.

Dr. Joya Uraizee, an Associate Professor of English at St. Louis University, spoke on "Representing the Horror of

Genocide." She stated that there are three kinds of literature relating to genocide. The first, she indicated, is by the survivors, which is not easy to share. They have problems telling a complete story. The second includes stories told by bystanders or observers, who often do not get the dates or sequence of particular events correct, though they do link the tragedy to the events. The third type is stories shared by scholars, who talk about ethnic cleansing. The details are accurate, but there is no personal content as what is true for one may not be for another. Uraizee stated that, "We are all human. Most people avoid speaking to other people about horrible events."

Uraizee further commented that, "Human rights are explained on where we need to pursue justice. This has not been done throughout Africa. The newer methods of law enforcement is being pursued and people will be captured and brought to justice for their crime."

Joseph Sebarenzi, who is a peace advocate and former speaker of the Rwandan parliament, stated, "As we commemorate, we need to go back and learn what took place, so that the horrible events such as a massacre will not be repeated. We need to build a better future, live in peace within ourselves."

During the Gathering, the history was briefly reviewed, which described how the Banyamulenge have been persecuted in the central region of Africa. In the 1990s genocide started and continued against the Banyamulenge people.

Dr. Harold Busch spoke on spirituality of grieving. He spoke regarding the "clouds of witnesses" related in Hebrews 12:1. This passage states:

"Therefore, since we are surrounded by such a great cloud of witnesses, let us throw of everything that hinders and the sin that so easily entangles, and let us run with perseverance the race marked out for us."

Dr. Busch reminded those gathered that, "We have respect and responsibility for the dead. The cross is the sign of great suffering." He further quoted Hebrews 12:2:

"Let us fix our eyes on Jesus, the author and perfecter of our faith, who for the joy set before him endured the cross, scorning it's shame, and sat down at the right hand of the throne of God."

Olivier Mandevu urged the people to tell their story of what happened that night, in 2004, when people were killed by guns and machetes and set on fire.

Jean Paul, a graduate of International Law from New Hampshire School of Law, is President of the Banyamulenge community in the United States and Canada. He spoke on the history of the Banyamulenge and shared information on the common ground of killing. He stated the ideal of ethnic cleansing is on the sole basis of ethnicity. "Men, women, children, soldiers, and older people of the Banyamulenge are being exterminated," he said. "No one has been persecuted by government and government officials. Justice needs to proceed on the criminals responsible for the extermination of innocent people of this tribe and others."

Later in the gathering, Angelique Ngendo shared her story of when she was shot in the hip during the massacre. She was seventeen years old when she saw a gunman inside her family's tent. Her father, sister, and brother were killed, and her mother was wounded in the shoulder. Angelique is now twenty-three and works as a housekeeper. She lives with her mother and other family members in Columbia, Missouri.

Esperance Nasezerano, who has a similar story, graduated from high school and plans to attend a community college in the fall. She stated she will always make time to connect with other survivors in future memorial gatherings.

Esperance Nasezerano stated, "It's a day to remember the past, and to know that the past won't come back."

Three hundred and fifty people attended the memorial gathering, and everyone enjoyed each other's company. The well-planned event was a success. There were lots of hugs and smiles as the survivors greeted one another throughout the gathering.

Memorial Service – Concorde, NH - 2009

Colorful dresses

More colorful dresses

Greeting friends

Fifth-year anniversary of the Gatumba Genocide
- David Byiringiro, Debbie Heagy and Laurent Muvunyi

Beatrice Nankumi - a survivor who
lost her left eye in Gatumba

The Gatuma Choir Foundation

Jolie Nyamukesha - Founder,
Gatumba Choir Foundation

The Attempted Refugee Camp Move

P astor John Bizimana, who visited Laurent in the late summer of 2009, had written letters from refugees to be sent to government officials in the United States voicing their concerns. Pastor Bizimana wrote his concerns regarding the movement of refugees and gave an itemized list, which I forwarded which I would forward in a letter to the senators of Ohio. I first had to find someone translate each letter from the refugees and from Pastor Bizimana, which were all in French, to English. Joyeuse Nambabazi, who attends Fairmont High School, knew a French teacher willing to help. Thus, I met with the teacher a few times to check on the progress of the translation of all the letters. I then composed a letter to Senator George Voinovich and Senator Sherrod Brown.

News was received that more than 400 Congolese refugees from a camp that was closed in Gihinga, Central Burundi, were stopped from entering their country. They were stopped by immigration officials of the Democratic Republic of Congo. The Burundion soldiers from the Mwaro Military Camp, together with the police, attacked the camp last Monday, at 4:00 a.m. in October, to force the refugee survivors to a different relocation facility[4]. The refugees were beaten and tortured by these men. The tents were destroyed by the Mwaro Military and the police. The refugees had to sleep outside.

The newly established refugee camp, Bwagiriza, is close to the border of Tanzania. The problem of being close to the rival tribe named the Babembe was the reason for not going to that camp. Also, the security is not guaranteed by the authorities of the Bwagiriza refugee camp. They house 1,200 people, which are mostly Congolese refugees.

The UNHCR and Burundi officials have been sending out information about the relocation. They were preparing the people for this move, but the Banyamulenge people were not too excited about the move. Senator George V. Voinovich graciously responded to the both my concerns from Kettering, Ohio, and those of Pastor John Bizimana. He stated that the Ghinga refugee camp had more that 2,000 refugees from the Banyamulenge community in the DRC. The United Nations High Commissioner for Refugees (UNHCR) tried to assure the refugees that there was a safe distance from the border of Tanzania.

The Banyamulenge people know too well when a move comes that they are the ones who get the short end of any opportunity. Their safety is not guaranteed anywhere they go. This gets old, and the spirits of these special people go down with continued disappointment. However, the Banyamulenge people are very religious, and they are strong. They just want to have a place they call home and to feel and be safe at night when they go to sleep. Included here are the letters sent and the response in detail from the letter of the senator.

---

[4] Georgianne Nienaber, Investigative journalist, Searcher and Author "Congo Spurns Burundi Refugees at Border" http://www.huffingtonpost. com/georgianne-nienaber/congo-spurns-burundi-refu.html (October 9, 2009 12:21PM)

September 21,2009

Debra Lynn Heagy
308 Earnshaw Drive
Kettering, Ohio 45429
(937) 620-6901

The Honorable Senator George Voinovich
524 Hart Senate Office Building
Washington DC 20510
(202) 224-3353

Dear Senator George Voinovich,

I am currently writing a book on "Voice of Central Africa" which focuses on genocide survivors of Gatamba in August of 2004 and other survivors of genocide in Central Africa.

Pastor John Bizimana flew from Central Africa to visit friends and share his testimony for the book I am currently writing. After this visit he will fly to New Hampshire for the 5th reunion of Gatamba massacre survivors who currently live in the United States for refuge and recovery which was held August 14th and 15th, 2009.

The pastor gave me letters from the refugees who are currently in refugee camps in Central Africa. Their concerns of being moved out of their camp. If these people are moved they will be subject to possible genocide which still prevails in this region. They will not be protected from danger and be exposed to possible fatalities.

Pastor John Bizimana further expressed the following concerns related to this point of interest. To transfer refugees is not good for them because there is no security and we ask the UN to intervene and protect the refugees. Then they can remain in Mwaro where it is secure or look for a way to transfer them to another country which would accept for them the refuge. He further adds the following information:

The Refugees' Transfer of Ghinga/Mwaro Camp to Bwagiriza and Ruyigi Camp
1. Because the opperationals and budget reasons, the Burundial Government, sponsors and UNHCR have decided that all Gihinga and Mwaro's refugees have to live in same camp or territory.
2. The camp of Gihinga is located at Kayokeve Commune in Mwaro Province and is holding a population of 2,529 persons.
3. There are two other congolese refugee camps located at Gasorwe Commune in Muyinga Province and Musaga Commune at Kiremba commune in Ngozi Province, are recently receiving new arrivals; they have the capacity of holding respectively 9,150 and 6390 persons.
4. The Competentes Administrative Authorities have accepted to offer another site and authorize to build or open a new camp of Bwagiriza at Kiremba Commune in Ruyigi Province. This site has 50 hectares and capacity of holding 9,000 persons.
5. Bwagiriza camp accepted since May 19,2009 to receive about 500 congolese refugees, those who are in transit to site of Songore in Ngozi Province and those who come from Bujumbura.
6. The Bwagiriza Camp has all conditions to protect and assist refugees before they return to their original countries. It will be the same instructions to Gihinga and other camps like Gasorwe as Musasa.
7. According to the next school openings, the Government of Burundi and UNHCR invited respectively all refugees to have a transfer inscription, which will start on August 15th to August 31st, 2009.

Thank you for your time and I hope you can help us with this special request. Enclosed with this letter is the letters from the refugees.

Sincerely Yours,

Debra Lynn Heagy

REPUBLIQUE DU BURUNDI   Gihinga, le 2./Juillet./2009
CAMP DE REFUGIES CONGOLAIS
DE GIHINGA/MWARO

Objet : Regret sur le déplacement
de réfugiés congolais du Camp
de Gihinga vers Ruyigi   A l'Excellence Mr, le Président
                                         de la République du Burundi
                                                    à
                                              BUJUMBURA

Excellence le Président,

Nous avons l'honneur de venir auprès de votre haute autorité en vue de vous présenter notre regret au message du Coordinateur de l'Office National de protection des réfugiés et Apatrides « ONAPRA », lors de sa dernière visite dans le Camp de Gihinga mardi, le 12 juin 2009, repris en objet de la présente.

En effet l'excellence le Président, permettez nous de vous raconter en grosso modo la façon dont nous avons été transférés dans ce Camp où nous sommes aujourd'hui. Lors de notre fuite au Congo vers le Burundi l'année 2004, un groupe de nos familles a été installé à Karurama/province cibitoke et un autre à Gatumba où les personnes ont été sauvagement massacrés près de la frontière de la République Démocratique du Congo. A la même période les tentatives d'attaques, de camp de Karurama par les malfaiteurs ont été entreprises contre nous. Pour nous, elles ont raté ceci pour dire que à Gatumba et Karurama nous étions exposés à la mort. Conformément aux lois régissant les réfugiés qui stipulent que les Camps des réfugiés ne pourraient jamais être placés près de la frontière de leur pays natal ; après que ce massacre ait eu lieu, le Gouvernement Burundais conjointement avec le H.C.R. avaient décidé de transférer tous les rescapés de ces réfugiés à GIHINGA dans la province de Mwaro situé au Centre du pays où la sécurité nous est totalement garantie. Chose qui nous étonne et celle d'entendre une décision brusque de nous transférer à Ruyigi près de la frontière de la Tanzanie, alors que la décision de la réunion du 4/septembre 2004, dans la quelle nos délégués ont pris part, avaient décidé que notre réinstallation sera définitive jusqu'au retour dans notre pays natal dans la Province du Katanga/Shaba

Enfin l'excellence le Président, pour cette inquiétude d'être exposé une fois de plus au massacre, la Tanzanie héberge nos ennemis Congolais qui gardent nos personnes (femmes et enfants) prises en otage de puis 1996 débuts de la guerre contre le Président Mobutu. Ainsi nous vous prions de revoir cette décision prise pour sécuriser les innombrables vies humaines, au cas contraire nous trouvons impossible de quitter Mwaro pour des raisons citées ci hauts.

Cependant, si le Burundi ne veut plus nous héberger au tant mieux nous préparer le rapatriement dans notre pays natal, ou de nous trouver un autre pays pouvant nous héberger et qui peut nous garantir la protection jusqu'à ce que la paix sera rétablie dans notre Pays.

Espérant que nos doléances seront bien écoutées, veuillez agréer l'excellence le Président de la République, l'expression de nos sentiments d'une profonde inquiétude.

Pour les réfugiés

C.P.I. à

- · L'Excellence le VICE-PRÉSIDENT de la République du Burundi
- · Madame la Représentante du H.C.R au Burundi à Bujumbura
- · Monsieur le Ministre de l'Intérieur et de la Sécurité Publique du Burundi
- · Monsieur le Minstre des affaires étrangères au Burundi
- · Monsieur le Représentant du H.C.R au Genève /Suisse
- · Monsieur le Coordinateur de l'ONAPRA
- · Monsieur le Représentant du Droit de l'Homme au Burundi
- · Monsieur le Gouverneur de la Province Mwaro
- · Monsieur le Représentant de LIGUE ITEKA au Burundi
- · Monsieur le chargé de la sécurité au H.C.R au Burundi
- · Madame chargée de la protection des réfugiés Mwaro.
- · Monsieur l'Administrateur du Camp de réfugiés de GIHINGA

Vous trouverez en annexe les noms et signatures des Représentants des réfugiés du camp de GIHINGA

REPUBLIQUE DU BURUNDI   Gihinga, le 28/Juillet/2009
CAMP DE REFUGIES CONGOLAIS
DE GIHINGA/MWARO
Tel : 79322775

Objet : Position de réfugiés congolais
Du camp de Gihinga /Mwaro
sur l'annonce de transfert vers BWAGIRIZA
Ruyigi

                          Madame la Représentante
                          du HCR au BURUNDI
                                   A
                          <u>BUJUMBURA</u>

Madame la représentante,

Nous avons l'honneur de nous adresser à votre haute autorité pour vous présenter notre vive préoccupation vis avis de la question de destruction du camp de réfugiés de GIHINGA au 31 Août 2009, au sein de votre institution dont la responsabilité vous est confiée.

En effet, Madame la Représentante,

Vu la dernière visite du 22/07/2009 de la Représentante Adjoint du HCR au Burundi et Coordinateur de l'ONPRA (79921351) pour nous annoncer la destruction de notre Camp et l'ouverture d'un autre camp à RUYIGI. Après votre visite tous les réfugiés s'étaient consultés et ont jugé bon de rentrer au Congo au lieu d'être transférés à RUYIGI pour des raisons citées ans la lettre du 2/juillet 2009. Après que le massacre de Katumba ait eu lieu, le Gouvernement Burundais conjointement avec le H.C.R. Avaient décidés de transférer tous les rescapés de ces réfugiés à GIHINGA dans la province de Mwaro situé au Centre du pays où la sécurité nous est totalement garantie. Sur ce, nous vous demanderions de toujours continuer à nous héberger à Mwaro au centre du pays où l'on est totalement sécurisés jusqu'à maintenant. Au cas où notre transfert se révélerait incontournable, nous vous demanderions de nous rapatrier au Congo dans la province de KATANGA avant le 2/septembre 2009 la date de l'ouverture de l'école à Ruyigi et fermeture des écoles à Mwaro selon l'annonce de l'ONPRA.

Nous vous prions Madame la Représentante, de croire nos sentiments le plus distingués dans l'attente d'une suite favorable et nous vous en remercions.

Copies pour information

- Gouvernement provincial du KATANGA (RDC)
- Commissaire sous régional du tanganyika (RDC)
- HCR au katanga (RDC)
- Ambassade de la RDC au BURUNDI
- MONUC au CONGO
- Coordinateur de l'ONPRA AU BURUNDI

Signataires en annexes

REPUBLIQUE DU BURUNDI   Gihinga, le 28/Juillet/2009
CAMP DE REFUGIES CONGOLAIS
DE GIHINGA/MWARO
Tel : 79322775

Objet : Protestation de transfert de réfugiés
Congolais du camp de Gihinga Mwaro
Vers le camps de BWAGIRIZA /RUYIGI

Transmis copies pour information à
- REPRESENTANT DE UNION EUROPEENNE AU BURUNDI
- REPRESENTANT DU BUNIB AU BURUNDI
- HONORABLE PRESIDENT DU SENAT AU BURUNDI
- HONORABLE PRESIDENT DE L'ASSEMBLEE NATIONALE AU BURUNDI
- AMBASSADEUR DES ETAS UNIS AU BURUNDI
- AMBASSADEUR DE FRANCE AU BURUNDI
- AMBASSADEUR DE BERGIQUE AU BURUNDI
- REPRESETANT DE PAYS BAS AU BURUNDI
- CONSULAT ROYAL DE NORVEGE AU BURUNDI
- CONSULAT DU CANADA AU BURUNDI
- PRESIDENT DE CNDD-FDD AU BURUNDI
- PRESIDENT DE L'UPRONA AU BURUNDI
- PRESIDENT DU FRODEBU AU BURUNDI
- PRESIDENT DU MRC AU BURUNDI
- PRESIDENT DU PARENA AU BURUNDI
- DROIT DE L'HOMME GITEGA
- LIGUE ITEKA AU BURUNDI
- APRODH AU BURUNDI
- ARCHEVEQUE DES EGLISES CATHOLIQUE AU BURUNDI
- ARCHEVEQUE DES EGLISES ANGLICANS
- CONSEIL NATIONAL DES EGLISES AU BURUNDI
- MONSEIGNEUR DE L'EGLISE ANGLICAN AU BURUNDI
- LE REPRESENTANT DA LA COMMUNAUTE MUSULMANE AU BURUNDI
- ONPRA

Représentant de l'Union Européenne,

Nous avons l'honneur de nous adresser à votre haute autorité pour vous présenter notre vive préoccupation vis avis de la question de destruction de camp de réfugiés de GIHINGA au 31 Août 2009. Nous avons été sidéré quand nous avons pris connaissance par le Coordinateur de l'ONPRA (office national de protection des réfugiés (79921351) de sa décision consistant à transférer le camp de Gihinga vers un nouveau site de Ruyigi (Bwagiriza) à la frontière de la Tanzanie.

En effet, le Représentant, le transfert de notre camp, les raisons avancées par le Coordinateur de l'ONPRA ne sont pas fondées selon nous car l'étendue où se trouve le Camp est vaste et non habitée, pour de raison économique notre camps est équipé de :

De plus de 500 maisonnettes,

Une école moderne construite en briques cuite,

3 gros stocks et robinet public suffisant,

Des latrines, douches et autres infrastructures non cités,

Notre préoccupation est celle-ci, comment pouvez-vous démolir des infrastructures déjà en place pour aller reconstruire ailleurs?

Signalons que la destruction pour nous les Réfugiés congolais BANYAMURENGE a été habituelle en bafouant l'article 26 et 33 de la convention et protocole relatif au statut de réfugiés, cas typique à NGAGARA 2002, RUGOMBO 2003, CISHEMERI 2004, KARURAMA 2004 toujours par le coordinateur de l'ONPRA . Sachant que nous avons été transférer à GIHINGA après que le massacre de Katumba où plus de 166 personnes (hommes, vieillards, femmes, enfants,   ) ont été sauvagement massacrés. La réunion du 4/septembre 2004 tenues par le Gouvernement Burundais conjointement avec le H.C.R. Avaient décidés de transférer tous les rescapés de ces réfugiés à GIHINGA dans la province de Mwaro situé au Centre du pays où cette réinstallation selon eux serait définitive jusqu'au retour dans notre pays natal dans la province du Katanga.

Sur ce, nous vous demanderions de toujours continuer à nous héberger à Mwaro au centre du pays où l'on est totalement sécurisés jusqu'à maintenant car RUYIGI est une province frontalière où nous craignons que notre vies seraient en danger de mort comme nos frères de GATUMBA. Au cas où notre transfert se révélerait incontournable, nous vous prions de nous rapatrier au Congo dans la province de KATANGA avant le 2/septembre 2009, la date de l'ouverture de l'école à Ruyigi et celle de fermeture des écoles à Mwaro selon l'annonce de l'ONPRA.

Nous vous prions les Représentants, de croire nos sentiments le plus distingués dans l'attente d'une suite favorable et nous vous en remercions.

Les signataires en annexes et la lettre d'annonce.

GEORGE V. VOINOVICH
OHIO

624 HART SENATE OFFICE BUILDING
(202) 224-3353
TDD: (202) 224-6997
http://voinovich.senate.gov

United States Senate

WASHINGTON, DC 20510-3504

APPROPRIATIONS
RANKING MEMBER, SUBCOMMITTEE ON
HOMELAND SECURITY

ENVIRONMENT AND
PUBLIC WORKS
RANKING MEMBER, SUBCOMMITTEE ON
TRANSPORTATION AND INFRASTRUCTURE

HOMELAND SECURITY AND
GOVERNMENTAL AFFAIRS
RANKING MEMBER, SUBCOMMITTEE ON
OVERSIGHT OF GOVERNMENT MANAGEMENT,
THE FEDERAL WORKFORCE, AND
THE DISTRICT OF COLUMBIA

November 4, 2009

Ms. Debra Heagy
308 Earnshaw Drive
Kettering, Ohio 45429

Dear Debra:

Thank you for contacting me regarding Congolese refugee camps in Burundi.

On September 30, 2009, the United Nations High Commissioner for Refugees (UNHCR) moved the Chinga refugee camp in central Burundi to the Bwagiriza camp in eastern Burundi. The Chinga camp contained more than 2,000 refugees from the Banyamulenge community in the neighboring Democratic Republic of the Congo (DRC). Many Congolese have refused to relocate to the Bwagiriza camp due to its proximity to what they claim is a Banyamulenge rival community in Tanzania. Although the UNHCR has assured the refugees that the Bwagiriza camp is at a safe distance from the Tanzania border, most refugees have stated they would rather return to the DRC.

On July 9, 2009, Senator Patrick Leahy (D-VT) introduced S. 1434, the Department of State, Foreign Operations, and Related Programs Appropriations Act, 2010. S. 1434 recommends $1.67 billion for Migration and Refugee Assistance for the suffering of all refugees and Internally Displaced Persons. S. 1434 passed the Senate Committee on Appropriations, of which I am a member, and has been placed on Senate Legislative Calendar.

I appreciate hearing from you on this issue and I welcome your views on this or any other issue that concerns you.

Sincerely,

George V. Voinovich

George V. Voinovich
United States Senator

STATE OFFICES:
36 EAST SEVENTH STREET
ROOM 2615
CINCINNATI, OHIO 45202
(513) 684-3265

1240 EAST NINTH STREET
ROOM 3061
CLEVELAND, OHIO 44199
(216) 522-7095

37 WEST BROAD STREET
ROOM 300
COLUMBUS, OHIO 43215
(614) 469-6697
(614) 469-6774 (CASEWORK)
(800) 205-6446 (CASEWORK)

78 WEST WASHINGTON STREET
P.O. BOX 57
NELSONVILLE, OHIO 45764
(740) 441-6410

420 MADISON AVENUE
ROOM 1210
TOLEDO, OHIO 43604
(419) 259-3895

PRINTED ON RECYCLED PAPER

List of Prisoners

The List of Prisoners in Bakita Jail Executed in Lubumbashi 1998

Nehemie Murondorwa
Semahoro Mujimbira
Ndayishimiye Biganiro
Bugabo Mureta
Moise Macumu
Munyamahoro Muberwa
Nyakintu Serushahi
Bunome Mubembe
President Mudagiri
Muhire Gatiritiri
Maso Ruramira
Mberwa Ntagwejera
Musabwa Gasigwa
Mbabazi Tundwa
Masomo Gatibita
Irakiza Rwambaza
Sadiki Rwakira
Kazungu
Bwiza Gatware
Mbonimpa Ndabagoye
Zakayo Butsiriko
Gatoki Murabya

Kadoni Kagurumoya
Mushonda Rwambukirana
Gasongo Yasosi
Patrick Kanyamurambu
Ntabaresha Gasuzuguro
Alexis Ntego
Gatonzi Gafurumba
Gedeon
Siraheri
Pasteur Murondorwa
Rukara Kabungurura
Mugabe
Gasongo
Kigeri Karema
Jacque Gatambara
Roger Semahoro
Nicola Bikoroti
Sungura Rwandikiye
Obed Alexis
Girbert Kabuye
Mutasti Sebambe
Mujabika Kabemba
Kibinda Karekezi
Runezerwa
Bahanda
Ezechiel Rugaza
John Sebagabo
Rumenge Rutihinda
Ruhumuriza Masiribo
Rugazura Kanyamararo
Muhinyuza
Gasongo Gishungu
Fils Rwakuranwa
Samuel Ngirumuvugizi
Rududu Rwemankuku

Tharasisi Gashabagizi
Jean P. Bizimana
Hakizimana
Murama
Dudu
Gacunda
Danton Nkumbuyinka
Fils Rushemwa
Serugo Mutwa
Bukuru Rwigimba
Munyakarama Rwihimba
Rusaha Rusanganirwa
Zikiya Ndahigirwa
Bideri Sekidende
Kanoro Sebatware
Kaniki Kanyamizingo
Rwiyereka Rutandara
Hakiza Nkundabatwre
Ndihano Bizuru
Simoni Sabune
Ndendechi Gitungano
Jean Marie Muhindanyi
Muhoza Gatembe
Kizehe Mudage
Munyaruhanga Bahirwa
Gasita Muhoza
Samuel Ndateba
Rugaraba Mukenga
Bizimana Rutaha
Mukiza Kabungurura
Gishahira Nyandinda
Daniel Rukuza
Kamayo Karimundoga
Mayunga Binono
Nehemiya Namajana

Mukamyi Mazimano
Ruhamya Mazimano
Mukwiza Rwumbuguza
Gadi Murondorwa
Masiribo
Kibinda
Osee Kamayo
Bideri Karekezi
Birume Banta
Mutunzi Honga
Zikiya
Nyamajana Murondorwa
Gadi Murondorwa
Manasse Rugaraba
Mubuga Runyakura

Courtesy of Narira Muzinga, who provided the list at Bakita Jail 1998

List of the Massacred: Gatumba Genocide
August 13 and 14, 2004

Faustin Minyati
Khadafi Minyati
Mereweneza Minyati
Nyanone Minyati
Jacques Rutekereza
Mushambaro Rutekereza
Igiraneza Rutekereza
Nyamasoso Rutekereza
Ndatabaye Rutekereza
Nyazahabu Rutekereza
Nyamuryango Rutekereza
Eraste Gasosi
Perusi Gasosi
Nyahumure Gasosi
Bahoza Gasosi
Dibora Gasosi
Karaha Nyamusore
Debora Nyamusore
Ntarutwa Nyamusore
Kayonga Nyamusore
Ngezayo Nyamusore
Bebe Nyamusore
Osee Rukamirwa
Marsiyana Rukamirwa
Nyakirayi Rukamirwa
Bisetsa Rukamirwa
Haizuru Rukamirwa (petit-fils)
Haizuru Rukamirwa (petite-fille)
Mugotwa Gatoni
Nyabyiza Gatoni
Debora Gatoni (Jumelle)
Aimee Gatoni (Jumelle)

Marisiyana Shemu
Esperance Shemu
Jeremie Shemu
Masigabona Shoni
Nyankazi Shoni
Musa Shoni
Amani Shoni
Nyahoza Kasa
Ziraje Kasa
Jeannette Kasa
Yvonne Kasa
Bebe Kasa
Thomas Bitati
Wabitati Bitati
Nyahoza Zaroti
Bebe Zaroti
Odiya Kanyabitabo
Neza Kanyabitabo
Nyamugisha Musafiri
Pasi Musafiri
Nyabihogo Gapingi
Claude Gapingi
Gisele Gapingi
Lydia Musafiri
Blaise Musafiri
Lea Mandevu
Muhorana Mandevu
Leon Mandevu
Birete Mandevu
Cheche Butoto
Fiston Butoto
Mupenzi Butoto
Nyabyinshi Muhire
Muhire Muhire Wa
Uziya Gashindi Mukwiye

Dando Mukwiye
Lucie Mukwiye
Daniel Mukwiye
Zera Gaturuturu
Tantine Gaturuturu
Nyabahiga Mugabe
Nyabirori Mugabe
Bea Mugabe
Paulina Ntwari
Jaenne Ntwari
Christina Nyagakobga
Bebe Nyagakobga
Ntonipetite-fille
Manuel Ngakaji
Nezia Kalala
Nyagazura Rukungugu
Felix Rukungugu
Kamariza Rukungugu
Murekatete Sebahire
Patrick Sebahire
Kadada Sebahire
Nyarukundo Muyengeza
Rusengo Muyengeza
Musore Muyengeza
Bukuru Maniragaba
Ndayisenga Maniragabe
Ange Maniragaba
Askophe Gishoma
Nkunda Gishoma
Niyonkuru Sekabunda
Fabier R Biguge
MInnocent Biguge
Didier Biguge
Mukarukwiza Runezerwa
Bosse Runezerwa

Bijoux Runezerwa
Elias Bitagura Muhimuzi
Munone Muhimuzi
Mereweneza Muhimuzi
Munezero Muvange
Edouard Muvange
Nyamaronko
Nyambo Nyamaronko
Jeanne Nyamaronko
Kagigi Nyamaronko (petite-fille)
Nabitanga Serugarukira
Nyantebuka Serugarukira
Manasse Runagana
Catherine Runagana
Mukobwa Runagana
Ntonia Gasungunu
David Gasungunu
Ngakazi Ignace
Tembasi Ngakazi
Mukobwa Munyakuri
Murora Rugeza
Odia Ndagiro
Bunana Gasore
Mado Gahakanyi
Gafita Nyamuvyeyi
Nyamunezero Zuzi
Kajeyi Ruganza
Ndayishimiye Muzuri
Nyamajana Rushaga
Nyangore Rugabo
Mombo Kazingo
Nyamatungo Seruhung
Sifa Mariya
Andre Ndakanirwa
Ngombe Rushemuka

Ngwabi Kalala
Bizimana
Michael Nzungu
Rusekeza
Nyantonesha
Ruhumuriza Nyakirindo
Afande Binyonyo
Zikama Unkwere Murore
Tchisekedi Semuhoza
Ndasarara Mugiraneza
Niyitanga Semugazanya
Lulinda Abwe
Delphine Byamonea
Regine Batubula
Aoci Leon
Nyapamba Sadi
Nyapamba Bahati
Bokeoi Asukulu
Echa Mbeleci
Lukele Wa Lukele
Angalisho Mambo
Sumali Evariste
Jeannette Kiza
Wisumbelo Isumbelo
Ndalo Namirenge

Source of the list: Laurent Muvunyi, Bujumbura Burundi 2005 three people are not listed; the total count is 164 who were killed in the Gatumba Genocide, August 13 and 14, 2004.

Current Status of the
Banyamulenge People

This update is courtesy of Ruramira B. Zebedee, a Rule of Law Officer UNDP/Recovery Program.

The current situation of the Banyamulenge people is not good. In the Villages of Uvira, in terms of security, they are occupied with soldiers who are not dealt by the government. They must live, eat, and get dressed in these villages. They live with the means of the population with all the unimaginable consequences; slaughters, rapes [sometimes collective of women and girls], robbery of the farm animals and cultures, sequestrations, arbitrary arrests . . . and the great part of them left their villages to try to save their own lives. They give up their fields, houses, grounds, and animals. Some of the people are scattered in the neighboring countries of Kenya, Uganda, Burundi, Rwanda without any hope to return one day to their own country. They are all lost. Banyamulenge do not move freely in the country without being killed by soldiers, peasants of other tribes or ethnic groups, or militia armed from Rwanda or the Congo. Poverty is lived every day.

The Banyamulenge have not been accepted by the government and the political extremists, such as Congolese citizens, throughout the centuries in the Congo. The future of the Banyamulenge will depend on the involvement of the following: the international community, especially the great powers and the neighboring countries of the DRCongo; and the Congolese government itself and of its will to live together with populations of the eastern portion of the Congo. In the absence of this involvement, the Banyamulenge people will be victims of extermination and disappearance as a people since the very recent history has proven this to be the current course. Measures must be taken to prevent the extermination of these people.

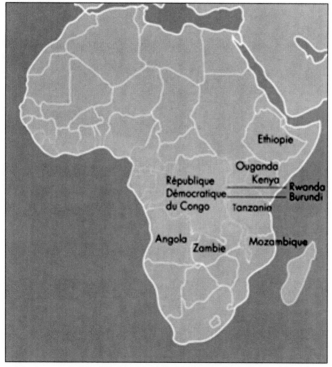

Map courtesy of: Ruramira B. Zebedee

The current refugee camps that house the Banyamulenge people in Rwanda are: Gihembe, Kiziba, Ngarama, and Nyagatare refugee camps.

181

The current refugee camps that house the Banyamulenge people in Burundi are: Muyinga, Mwaro, Ngagara, and Bujumbura refugee camps.

The current refugee camps that house the Banyamulenge people in Uganda are: Nakivale, Kyaka, Kampala, and Mbarara refugee camps.

The current refugee camp that houses the Banyamulenge people in Kenya is the Nairobi refugee camp.

Current Status on the Education System in the Banyamulenge Community

The following information is courtesy of Alexis Mbagariye Rwemera.

The education system in the Banyamulenge community has been one of the most challenging tasks of all time. First, given the geographical situation of Mulenge, being located in the high plateau of Uvira (3,000 meters altitude), there is no access to roads, electricity, or any other infrastructure. As a result, the education system, as well as other indicators of development, has proven to be very poor.

Second, from the early part of 1996 to the present, the Mulenge area has been somewhat a warzone. Consequently, no well-built education is taking place. Instead, young people roam all over Central African refugee camps. Some of them join either the government military or a dissident group, or they simply become involved in regional illegal activities.

Third, historically, the Banyamulenge tribe has been cattle herdsmen, which means that all that matters for them is simply a green pasture for their cows. Not much attention was given to anything else until recently in the 1980s.

Fourth, the place known as Zaire, which currently the DRCongo political environment, has been very hostile and discriminatory to some people, including the Banyamulenge. The educational system, as well as the whole government, was and is still very corrupt. It is broken so greatly that if an individual does not have enough private money to go to college there is no recourse through public/state funds or international scholarships.

In spite of great hardship, many of the Banyamulenge people did manage to go to school. Some became very successful, including their first elected member of parliament, the late Gisaro Muhoza, who was the first college graduate. Also of the Banymulege, the former Vice-President of the DRCongo, Mr. Azarias Ruberwa, was a lawyer per profession. Also included are many national senators, members of parliament, and vice-governors.

One would wonder why the Banyamulenge people lived in the Congo for over 400 years, and the answer is simply that there were no role models, no motivational speakers, and no perceived incentives to spend time studying. The people believed that all that mattered was to take care of cows and get married to produce a good number of children. There was almost a decade between the first graduate from college Mr. Gisaro Muhoza, in the 1970s until the Banyamulenge produced another college graduate. Muhoza at last showed the importance of school and began the institutionalized school system in the high plateau of Mulenge. From the early 1980s, the Banyamulenge had several high schools, and now there are even one to two private colleges.

"In total," Alexis Mbagariye Rwemera stated, "we may count twenty high schools and approximately 100 primary schools. However, the challenge we are facing is that we are still behind in terms of school material: no books, no chalk, no blackboards, no electricity, no durable buildings, no computers, no roads, no trained teachers, no salary, nothing except very few private schools that are trying to improve little by little. Imagine in the 21st century, schools without blackboards and chalk, or books."

In the entire community, only about ten individuals have received a Ph.D., and less than 100 have received master's degrees. Rwemera stated, "We can give credit to the government of Rwanda, which helped all immigrant Banyamulenge to go to school without any discrimination.

However, we have proven to be among the brightest and to build more schools of all times compare to our neighboring tribes who live under the same circumstances as our own. Now, we have a firm belief in the education system as the most powerful tool to change our world.

"Therefore, we urge the DRCongo government, and our country, to consider the forgotten tribe of the Banyamulenge as well as other minorities underserved for national scholarships and to seek international scholarships to study abroad, a chance we never had, unlike other tribes, because of discrimination, which we can't allow to keep continuing. Our children, instead of going to study in other countries . . . are scattered all over the neighboring countries in the refugee camps without education [and] therefore without a promising future.

"Finally, we urge the United States government, all international educational institutions, and private institutions to consider scholarships for minority tribes underserved, including the Banyamulenge tribe."

The Current Economic Status of the Banyamulenge Community

The following excerpt is courtesy of Claude Rwaganje, Executive Director of Community Financial Literacy:

The majority of the Banyamulenge live in the Eastern Congo in the high mountain of Mulenge. These villages are far from the city. The closest village is 100 miles. The nature of these villages is very good for cows; that's why they call them "Peuple Pastors" meaning, "farmers with many cows."

In terms of a financial institution, there is no single bank in these villages. When someone sells his cow, he will keep his money in the house, under a mattress. Men, not women, own cows. If a women was a widow who was left with any wealth, she would have to have someone in the family to help her in the decision-making process.

In terms of having access to a bank account, you have to travel more than 100 miles to find a bank, and even then, the Democratic Republic of Congo financial institution is generally broken or nonfunctioning. The people are not motivated to travel this distance to go to open an account as there is no advantage in owning a bank account.

Many Banyamulenge who have relocated to the United States still have a bad image of banks. This is why newcomers need training. The Banyamulenge who have been living in the United States at least for a year do understand that having a bank account will help them build a trusting relationship with a bank, which will in turn help them get a loan, build a good credit score, and get a loan at a low interest rate.

The Current Health Status of the Banyamulenge Community

The history from the survivors who had gunshot wounds and other ailments is, and always will be, a vivid memory of their scars resulting from genocide. The lack of health clinics and safe places of refuge create numerous ongoing problems for these people. The incidence of disease and infection causes a higher death rate among the African community.

Hopefully, in the future, health clinics will be built and medical staff can safely practice and provide adequate healthcare for the community. The availability of medicine to treat infections and disease will lower the incidence of death for easily-treated conditions.

The following statement is provided by Dr. Norbert Runyambo regarding health in the Congo, especially the Banyamulenge Tribe. Dr. Runyambo is a Physician Graduate from the Democratic Republic of Congo who worked twenty-eight years as a general practitioner at several places in hospitals in South Kivu [1979-2004].

"During the last five years (1999-2004) before I moved to the USA, I coordinated programs in the health centers throughout the province and worked with coordinators and physicians to improve national public health in DRCongo. The South Kivu has five million people from different tribes, including the Banyamulenge Tribe. The health situation has big issues, not only for the Banyamulenge Tribe, but for all tribes as well.

"The people of DRCongo have suffered violent war that took around four million people, according to United Nations' estimation, over ten years of the war. The South Kivu province is the most affected by violence and poverty. HIV, malnutrition, raped women, epidemic and endemic diseases have affected Congolese people during thirty-five years of dictatorship of Mobutu and fifteen years of the war. Therefore, from the 1960s the government did not really take value or interest in current health issues.

"What has happened regarding the Healthcare in Plateau of Uvira (Minembwe area): The community has a lot of problems, such as accessibility to the primary healthcare, the logistic problem due to long distance without roads, lack of medical staff, lack of medicine, no vaccines, no medical equipment, buildings that are destroyed, and even the security is a big issue in the area. Many people have tuberculosis and suffer with gastritis; immunization is big issue by lack of an efficiency of personnel and equipment. Education, especially in the medical field, is rare. We started Primary Care, but few nurses accepted to live in the area, [and] we were forced to use unqualified agents to help people. From 2001 we created hospitals in the area to properly cover the population and devised them in the three zones, so we were trying to provide adequate healthcare for every family.

HIV/AIDS: The number of people infected and affected by HIV/AIDS is the same in all tribes in the province (6-8%), malnourished (16%), safe water access (45%), respiratory tract infections, malaria, enteritis, leprosy, diabetes, TB, raped women [rape is not in control and continues to be a concern], access to maternity [care] (35%), efficiency immunization (45%).

"The need of healthcare is still big in the community, especially in the Banyamulenge area, with challenges of access. [We need to] obtain medical team staff, materials, medicine, education for local teams and new buildings. As one of the team, I recommend the Congo government to take the healthcare at a more serious level for all tribes."

Nyabiheke Refugee Camp in Rwanda

Small tent for orphans

Trying to make things like home

Looking for wood to burn for cooking meals

Covering tents with mud

A weathered tent

Trying to plant a garden

Home for now

Laundry day

Early stages of building a new home

Refugee village

Home inside of a tent before
the massacre at Gatumba

Conclusion

I enjoyed working on the book with Laurent, and I look forward to sharing this true and valid information from the Banyamulenge community with the world. Each person gave me permission to use his or her story in the book. I wish to thank everyone who contributed time and resources to provide information for the creation of this book, *Voice of Central Africa (DRCongo)*.

CPSIA information can be obtained at www.ICGtesting.com
Printed in the USA
BVOW012351110312

284863BV00001B/2/P